The Vision of the
Ecumenical
Movement
and
How It Has Been
Impoverished
by Its Friends

The Vision of the Ecumenical Movement
and
How It Has Been Impoverished by Its Friends

Michael Kinnamon

CHALICE PRESS

ST. LOUIS, MISSOURI

Cover design: Mike Foley
Cover art: Ship symbol from the World Council of Churches
Interior design: Hui-chu Wang
Art direction: Michael Domínguez

Visit Chalice Press on the World Wide Web at
www.chalicepress.com

10 9 8 7 6 5 4 3 2   07   08   09   10   11   12

Library of Congress Cataloging–in–Publication Data

Kinnamon, Michael.
  The vision of the ecumenical movement and how it has been impoverished by its friends / Michael Kinnamon.
      p. cm.
  Includes bibliographical references and index.
  ISBN-13: 978-0-827240-06-3 (alk. paper)
  ISBN-10: 0-827240-06-6 (alk. paper)
  1. Ecumenical movement–History. I. Title.
  BX6.5.K56 2003
  262'.001'1–dc21

                                                          2003000777

Printed in the United States of America

Contents

Dedication

This book is dedicated to the many colleagues in state and local councils of churches with whom I have worked in recent years. More than thirty state councils have invited me to think aloud with them about the vision and practice of ecumenism, and I am grateful for these opportunities—and for the friendships that have stemmed from them. I know that leadership in a local or state council of churches can, at times, be lonely and frustrating. This makes me all the more appreciative of these persons whose commitment to the gospel, and to the vision of a church united and renewed, keeps them in such positions.

Introduction

My direct involvement in the ecumenical movement began in 1980 when I joined the staff of the World Council of Churches (WCC) in Geneva, Switzerland. My particular responsibilities, as a member of the staff in Faith and Order, included work with united and uniting churches, preparation of materials for the Week of Prayer for Christian Unity, and participation in a study project known as the Community of Women and Men in the Church. I could hardly ignore, however, the attacks that were then being leveled at the Council as a whole, largely because of its moral and financial support for black liberation struggles in southern Africa.

I was admittedly a newcomer to this arena; but even to me the critiques seemed, at best, to lack nuance and, at worst, to be maliciously misguided. Yes, the World Council and other ecumenical organizations make pronouncements that challenge Western culture. But such pronouncements are not the product of a Geneva bureaucracy; they are the result of dialogue among representatives of the global church. Yes, the Council takes stands on political issues of the day. But doesn't obedience to Christ demand that his followers stand boldly against racism or economic exploitation? I could already see problems within the WCC, but these critiques missed the target.

Many of the criticisms of the WCC, and the ecumenical movement, were summarized in a widely discussed article that appeared in a 1982 issue of *Reader's Digest*.[1] The author identified two World Council leaders as representative of the Council's purported leftward tilt: Philip Potter, who was then the WCC's general secretary, and Emilio Castro, Potter's eventual successor who in 1982 was director of the WCC's Commission on World Mission and Evangelism. Readers were told that Potter is "fond of citing Marxist writers," but no mention was made of his passion for, and extraordinary knowledge of, the Bible. It is easy to dismiss people you don't know, but I knew this man to be a defender of the poor precisely because of his commitment to the gospel. The author of the

---

[1]Joseph A. Harriss, "Karl Marx or Jesus Christ?" *Reader's Digest* (August 1982): 130–34.

Reader's Digest article was either blinded by ideology or simply had no clue.

I was also aware that Castro had spoken with *Reader's Digest* for two hours, out of which the article used twelve words: "The philosophical basis of capitalism is evil, totally contrary to the gospel." There was no mention of Castro's marvelous gift for preaching or of his vigorous commitment to evangelization ("Christians owe the message of God's salvation in Jesus Christ to every person and every people"). I knew this man. *Reader's Digest* was way off base.

My distrust of such critics was reinforced when Carl McIntyre picketed our 1982 meeting of the Faith and Order Commission in Lima, Peru. His public statements made it sound as if the Council were only interested in promoting social revolution; our agenda focused on baptism, eucharist, ministry, and the church's confession of the apostolic faith. Then came the protests at the WCC's 1983 assembly in Vancouver led by such persons as Ian Paisley and Lyndon LaRouche. Most of the signs read "WCC Finances 'Reds'" (or a variation on that theme). But I vividly recall one demonstrator whose placard had a more theological message: "The KGB is an agent of the Russian Orthodox Church and its intention is to remove the filioque clause from the Creed"! With enemies like that, I can remember thinking, the ecumenical movement must be in pretty good shape.

Over the past eighteen years I have come to realize, however, that the ecumenical movement, despite notable achievements, is not in good shape. But the real threat never came from those protesting outside. It came and comes from within.

The single biggest problem facing the ecumenical movement (and the World Council of Churches), in my judgment, is a widespread failure to grasp and teach the biblically based vision of the church and its relationship to the world that gave energy and direction to ecumenical work throughout most of the twentieth century. Of course, this vision must be enlarged and modified and differently expressed in different eras and cultural contexts (a point I will emphasize in the final chapter of this book). But I am convinced (1) that there is, nonetheless, a coherent, compelling vision, discernible in the movement's primary documents and the writings of its key leaders, and (2) that this vision has been domesticated by the churches involved in the movement, impoverished by those of us who are ostensibly its supporters. The WCC's first general secretary, Willem Visser't Hooft, noted in the 1950s that "the ecumenical movement itself is in danger as long as its deepest intentions are not understood by the great mass of church [persons]."[2] Today, I fear that the original intentions and assumptions of the movement are little understood even by many of the churches' leaders.

Actually, this concern about vision is heard a lot these days in ecumenical meetings, including the Eighth Assembly of the WCC, held in Harare, Zimbabwe, in December of 1998. At that assembly, the moderator of the Council's Central Committee, Aram I of the Armenian Orthodox tradition, argued that "unless the churches re-own the ecumenical movement, and re-articulate clearly its vision by making it relevant to the life of the people, the ecumenical movement may lose its vitality and sense of purpose."[3] The WCC's current general secretary, Konrad Raiser, also called for a "rekindling of the vision" in a way that addresses the situation of the churches on the eve of a new millennium. In an interview with *The Christian Century,* Raiser put it this way:

> I wouldn't say that the vision that inspired the ecumenical movement of the past decades—the vision that centered on key concepts like unity, mission and evangelism, common witness, sharing and service, development—is not valid anymore. But it is sometimes couched in a language that does not easily relate to the everyday reality of people in the churches.[4]

This surely is a problem, but fresh language will not be sufficient if the basic vision is misconstrued. Such misconstrual is the subject of this book.

This complaint, of course, is not new; visions are often misunderstood. If this book had been written in an earlier era, however, it would undoubtedly have named the distortions differently. At one time, for example, there was a need to insist that unity is not a synonym for structural merger, but that red herring no longer requires response. Visser't Hooft spends several pages in his book *The Pressure of Our Common Calling* (1959) rejecting the "as if theory" (live now "as if" the church were actually united), which only serves, as he sees it, "to create

---

[2]W. A. Visser't Hooft, "The Ground of Our Unity," in *The Nature of the Unity We Seek,* ed. Paul S. Minear (St. Louis: Bethany Press, 1958), 121. References to humanity have been changed, as indicated, to reflect contemporary sensitivity to inclusive language. Quotations have also been altered to reflect contemporary rules for the use of capital letters.

[3]Diane Kessler, ed., *Together on the Way: Official Report of the Eighth Assembly of the World Council of Churches* (Geneva: WCC, 1999), 65.

[4]"Rearticulating an Ecumenical Vision: An Interview with Konrad Raiser," *The Christian Century* (May 12, 1993): 516.

the wrong impression that a utilitarian relationship is an adequate response to the call which God addresses to his church and to the need of the world."[5] I will raise a related concern in chapter 2, but the language of "as if" no longer figures prominently in ecumenical discussion.

There is an obvious danger in a book such as this. Dana Trilling once noted that part of the tragedy of McCarthyism is that it made it impossible for serious-minded people to criticize communism. You didn't dare give even implicit support to McCarthy's outrageous attacks. In the same way, I am a little uneasy about the pages that follow lest they give real ammunition to *Reader's Digest* or the Institute for Religion and Democracy or other opponents of the ecumenical movement. I am also convinced, however, that an unwillingness to face the movement's problems head-on may be the greatest impoverishment of all.

* * *

As the preceding pages probably indicate, I hope that this book finds an audience among "ecumenical insiders," persons who are already involved in, and knowledgeable about, the ecumenical movement. May it stir up discussion, even controversy, regarding the vision that informs our work. May it change the way we think about both the history of the movement and its future agenda. Where needed, may it rekindle a passion for our calling. Thirty years ago, Ernst Lange offered such a challenge to insiders in what I regard as one of the most insightful books ever written about ecumenism, *And Yet It Moves.* May this volume stand in that tradition!

The book is also intended, however, for persons who are new to the whole idea of an ecumenical church. I have tried to write the book in a way that is accessible for congregational study groups, councils of churches workshops, ministers' retreats, and seminary courses. With that in mind, a brief introduction to the history and structures of the ecumenical movement is included as appendix 1. Readers without an extensive background in ecumenism may wish to consult it before beginning chapter 1. I have also added a selection of the ecumenical movement's most important documents, which may be found in appendices 2–11.

---

[5]W. A. Visser't Hooft, *The Pressure of Our Common Calling* (Garden City, N.Y.: Doubleday, 1959), 18.

I also hope that clarity of vision will help expand the circle of the ecumenical movement's active participants. Many evangelical Christians, if I'm not mistaken, have steered clear of groups and discussions labeled "ecumenical" because of their perception that the movement pursues unity by compromising truth or pursues a political agenda at the expense of Christian faith. Some Orthodox Christians have accused the ecumenical movement of backing away from its historic commitment to church unity. Many liberal Christians have turned elsewhere out of a sense that ecumenism deals with anachronistic disputes rather than urgent questions of justice and inclusivity. Perhaps the approach taken in this book can provide new avenues for contact and conversation.

* * *

Despite the book's somewhat negative title, far more space is devoted to a positive statement of the vision than to specific examples of its impoverishment. If readers familiar with the ecumenical movement find that parts of my argument do not ring true to their experience, that my claims about impoverishment seem overstated or misdirected, then so be it. I would love to be wrong in my assessment of the current state of the movement! Generally speaking, I do not identify the problems I name with any particular person or group. If the vision of the ecumenical movement has been distorted or misunderstood, then all of us who are involved in ecumenical work, certainly myself included, need to take responsibility for its recovery. We need shared reflection, not finger pointing.

Other facets of the ecumenical vision could have been included in this study. There are two in particular that I seriously considered for additional chapters.

1. The ecumenical vision is concerned with the visible unity of the church, a unity tangible enough that it makes a witness to the world of God's power to reconcile. The first purpose of the World Council of Churches, according to its Constitution, is "to call the churches to the goal of visible unity in one faith and one eucharistic fellowship expressed in worship and common life in Christ, and to advance towards that unity in order that the world may believe."[6] According to Visser't Hooft, "...one of the basic discoveries of ecumenical history [is] that the *una sancta* [the one, holy church] is not a beautiful ideal, but a God-given reality which

---

[6]In Michael Kinnamon and Brian E. Cope, eds., *The Ecumenical Movement: An Anthology of Key Texts and Voices* (Geneva: WCC; Grand Rapids, Mich.: Eerdmans, 1997), 469.

demands concrete manifestation."[7] After all, the opposite of visible unity is visible disunity—which, I fear, is how we Christians look to our neighbors. The way we live in community should lead others to ask: "What enables you to care so for one another even when you are so apparently different?"

There are Christians, of course, who deny or minimize the importance of visible unity, arguing that the unity spoken of in scripture does not require external form. I recently received a booklet published by a group that is opposed to Churches Uniting in Christ, a new covenantal relationship among nine U.S. Protestant denominations (discussed more fully in chapter 2). The churches' unity, according to the booklet's author, "doesn't have to be negotiated or organized by denominational officials. It is a spiritual unity recognized by all mature Christians." Such statements, however, generally come from those who would not consider themselves "friends" of the ecumenical movement. Within the movement itself, there is broad agreement that visibility, of some sort, is a necessary characteristic of the unity we seek.

There is an impoverishment, however, that must be named: that is, settling for a "unity" that isn't costly, for church relationships that don't make much of a witness because they don't demand much change. Concern over this issue runs throughout the book, especially in the final section of chapter 2.

2. The vision of the ecumenical movement contends that local fellowship and mission and global fellowship and mission are radically impoverished if separated from one another. A classic formulation is the definition of unity set forth by the WCC's New Delhi Assembly in 1961. What we envision, said the delegates, is a fully committed fellowship of "all in each place...who at the same time are united with the whole Christian fellowship in all places and all ages."[8] Ernst Lange, in *And Yet It Moves,* suggests that ecumenism has a "basis to universality."[9] Participants in the movement seek to expand the circle of our active empathy beyond ourselves, our neighborhoods, our denominations, our nations to include the *oikoumene* (a Greek term, from which "ecumenical" is derived, meaning "the whole inhabited earth"). But ecumenical texts usually add in the same breath that this global vision must be embodied in local communities of intense, visible relationships.

---

[7] In Kinnamon and Cope, 42.

[8] In Kinnamon and Cope, 88.

[9] Ernst Lange, *And Yet It Moves: Dream and Reality of the Ecumenical Movement,* trans. Edwin Robertson (Grand Rapids, Mich.: Eerdmans, 1979), 156.

It is always difficult to hold these together. Few ecumenical participants pay equal attention to the local and the global. But, finally, I don't see misunderstanding among friends of the movement about the necessity of this tension. Our practice may be impoverished, but not really our vision.

Perhaps the greatest contemporary impoverishment doesn't fit my chapter format because it has to do with every issue I will discuss: namely, the loss of theological depth and conviction that marks so many churches, at least in the West. In the fall of 1998, I participated in a largely unstructured seminar, involving thirty ecumenical "veterans," on the future of the movement. To the surprise of many of us, the dominant theme of the seminar turned out to be what one Catholic participant called "the erosion of the [theological] basis." If you don't believe that God has indeed acted in Christ for the salvation of the world, then the idea that God has created a new community in Christ of Jew and Gentile, as a sign and instrument of God's mission, will seem like pure idealism—impossible and, ultimately, irrelevant. In the absence of such conviction, ecumenism will become simply another arena for pursuing political agendas. Mark Heim summarized our conversations this way in an article for *The Christian Century*:

> This uncertainty [about what the church confesses] can shift the focus in ecumenical theology strongly toward the notion that unity is something we accomplish rather than a gift already manifest in Christ who embraces us all, even as we recoil from each other. On the other hand, this "erosion" can foster a readiness to simply declare unity in our current diversity. The most minimal terms of oneness are then taken as all that could be necessary.[10]

And when either happens, the church is impoverished.

---

[10]S. Mark Heim, "Something to Declare," *The Christian Century* (December 9, 1998): 1174–75.

— 1 —

Unity as Gift

Why Communion Is Not Our Achievement

At the heart of the ecumenical movement is the conviction that there *is* one church and that its members, however fragmented they may seem, are deeply related to one another thanks to what God has done in Jesus Christ. The ecumenical task, therefore, is not to create unity, but to address divisions of human origin in order that the unity God has given may be visible to the world.

These claims are often supported in the literature of the movement by a number of obvious biblical texts. The letter to the Ephesians, for example, proclaims that Jews and Gentiles have been reconciled in Christ, have been made members together in the household of God (Ephesians 2:19). Christians are enjoined "*to maintain* the unity of the Spirit in the bond of peace." For "there *is* one body and one Spirit...one Lord, one faith, one baptism, one God and Father of all, who is above all and through all and in all" (Ephesians 4:3–6). In a sense, however, such prooftexting misses the point. In the words of the Second World Conference on Faith and Order (Edinburgh, 1937), "*Everything* that the New Testament says about the church presupposes its fundamental unity"[1]–which is why unity is made an article of faith in the Nicene Creed. By definition, the church is holy, catholic, apostolic–and one.

---

[1]Leonard Hodgson, ed., *The Second World Conference on Faith and Order* (New York: MacMillan, 1938), 235.

The way Christians live, however, generally belies this confession. Relationships among the followers of Christ are frequently marked by competition or indifference or suspicion. Differences of belief and practice mean that parts of the church are divided at the Lord's table and unable to recognize the validity of each other's ministries. Differences of race, nation, culture, and class have led to separate communities whose relationship is often one of neglect rather than the hospitality of brothers and sisters. In our own era, Christians continue to kill other Christians in the name of political or ethnic loyalties.

It should not be surprising, therefore, that scripture not only affirms the essential unity of Christ's body but repeatedly admonishes Christians *to be* what they *are*. According to John's gospel, for example, Jesus instructed his disciples to be a community of visible love (John 13:12–17) and prayed that they "may all be one" in order "that the world may believe that you [the Father] have sent me" (John 17:21). In this sense, the unity of the church is not only a gift but a calling.

One of the leading contemporary ecumenists, Harding Meyer, speaks of this as the ecumenical indicative ("It is God who assembles the one church") and the ecumenical imperative (Christians must "give expression to the oneness of the church of Jesus Christ").[2] This dialectic of indicative-imperative, as Meyer points out, is the structure of Pauline thought. "If we live in the Spirit [which we do], let us also walk in the Spirit" (Galatians 5:25). If we are one in Christ (which we are), let us also live and act as a reconciled people.

It is surely an impoverishment of the ecumenical vision to minimize the severity or significance of church division, which, in the words of the Second Vatican Council, "openly contradicts the will of Christ, scandalizes the world, and damages that most holy cause, the preaching of the gospel to every creature."[3] If Christians fail to address the visible signs of such separation, then they are not living ecumenically—no matter how much they may affirm that they are "one in the Spirit." But an even greater impoverishment is the failure to recognize that unity is God's achievement, already accomplished in Christ. The imperative— to work, with the help of the Spirit, to realize tangible Christian

---

[2]Harding Meyer, *That All May Be One: Perceptions and Models of Ecumenicity*, trans. William G. Rusch (Grand Rapids, Mich.: Eerdmans, 1999), 9–13.

[3]"Decree on Ecumenism," in *The Ecumenical Movement: An Anthology of Key Texts and Voices*, ed. Michael Kinnamon and Brian E. Cope (Geneva: WCC; Grand Rapids, Mich.: Eerdmans, 1997), 27.

communion—stems from the indicative. Or as the ecumenical leader, Philip Potter, once put it, "What we are we must become."[4]

One of the great early statements of the vision of the ecumenical movement is the "Affirmation of Union in Allegiance to Our Lord Jesus Christ" from the 1937 Faith and Order conference referred to above. (See appendix 4 for this document.) Our unity, it states,

> does not consist in the agreement of our minds or the consent of our wills. It is founded on Jesus Christ himself, who lived, died and rose again to bring us to the Father, and who through the Holy Spirit dwells in his church. We are one because we are all the objects of the love and grace of God, and called by him to witness in all the world to his glorious gospel.[5]

The "Message" from the World Council's first assembly (Amsterdam, 1948) puts it more succinctly: "Christ has made us his own and he is not divided."[6] (See appendix 5 for this document.) Four years later, at the Third World Conference on Faith and Order in Lund, Sweden, Oliver Tomkins insisted that the implication of our "given unity in Christ" is that churches "should do together everything except what irreconcilable difference of sincere conviction compels us to do separately."[7] Slightly revised, this sentence came to be known as the Lund Principle—one of the most widely quoted, if still not practiced, axioms of modern ecumenism.

This theme found perhaps its fullest expression, however, in the famous definition of unity written by the WCC's third assembly (New Delhi) in 1961: "We believe that the unity which is both *God's will* and *God's gift* to his church is being made visible as all in each place who are baptized in Jesus Christ and confess him as Lord and Savior are brought by the Holy Spirit into one fully committed fellowship."[8] This unity, said the assembly report, is the unity of the triune God.

> It is the unity which he gives to his people through his decision to dwell among them and to be their God. It is the unity which he gives to his people through the gift of his Son, who by his death and resurrection binds us together in him in his Sonship

---

[4]Philip Potter, *Life in All Its Fullness* (Geneva: WCC, 1981), 37.
[5]In Kinnamon and Cope, 85.
[6]In Kinnamon and Cope, 21.
[7]Oliver S. Tomkins, ed., *The Third World Conference on Faith and Order* (London: SCM Press, 1953), 170.
[8]In Kinnamon and Cope, 88.

to the one Father. It is the unity given to his people through his Spirit, and through all the gifts of the Spirit which enliven, edify and empower the new humanity in Christ.[9]

Notice that the New Delhi Statement, as it is called, identified two external marks of participation in the one church that is God's gift: baptism in Jesus Christ and confession of him as Lord and Savior. There may be instances when a community is judged by other churches to be outside the circle of Christian fellowship despite having these marks (e.g., the Church of Jesus Christ of Latter Day Saints or the apartheid-supporting churches in South Africa), but we start with the presumption of relatedness. Christians involved in the ecumenical movement obviously seek to go far beyond these marks to a life of full sacramental sharing and common mission, but such "achievements" (which are themselves, we confess, evidence of the Holy Spirit) are possible only because we are branches of the same life-giving vine.

This point appears repeatedly in the essays and speeches of such ecumenical pioneers as Nathan Söderblom, William Temple, Suzanne de Dietrich, D. T. Niles, and, especially, the WCC's first general secretary, Willem Visser't Hooft. "We do not come together," wrote Visser't Hooft in a typical passage, "as people who have to begin by finding a common foundation for their relationship. That foundation has been laid. The starting point is given. We seek *koinonia* [communion, fellowship] because there is *koinonia* in our common submission to Christ."[10] Visser't Hooft distinguished between the given unity that holds us together now and the promised fuller unity for which we work and pray, but the latter would be literally unthinkable without a recognition of the former. This, argued Albert Outler, is precisely what makes the modern ecumenical movement "significantly different from the hundred ecumenical projects in the past three centuries which have started bravely—and failed!…Modern ecumenism begins with *the present fact of our unity in Christ.*" This assumption of initial mutual commitment is, in Outler's judgment, "the essential precondition for ecumenical discussion, worship and expectation,"[11] because it

---

[9]W. A. Visser't Hooft, ed., *The New Delhi Report: The Third Assembly of the World Council of Churches* (New York: Association Press, 1962), 118.

[10]W. A. Visser't Hooft, *The Pressure of Our Common Calling* (Garden City, N.Y.: Doubleday, 1959), 73.

[11]Albert C. Outler, *The Christian Tradition and the Unity We Seek* (London: Oxford University Press, 1958), 10, 24.

tempers the inclination to begin by attacking other churches while defending our own.

I especially appreciate Archbishop Temple's formulation: "We could not seek union if we did not already possess unity. Those who have nothing in common do not deplore their estrangement. It is because we are one in allegiance to one Lord that we seek and hope for the way of manifesting that unity in our witness to him before the world." It is because they are one in Christ that Christians feel the pain of a broken Table. It is because we are one in Christ that we lament the scandal of competing denominations. It is because we are one in Christ that we seek to overcome our divisions of whatever cause. And if we do draw closer to one another, said Temple, "then our task will be not to consummate our endeavor but to register [God's] achievement."[12]

* * *

I need to acknowledge that representatives of the Orthodox churches have often expressed difficulty with this formulation of the ecumenical vision. Orthodox theologians agree that unity belongs to the church's essential, God-given nature. But this unity, they contend, cannot be made visible through what one Orthodox statement calls "inter-denominational adjustment."[13] The unity of the one church has been broken and must be recovered, not through a mutual recognition of various denominations but through a return to the Tradition of the apostles (to which the Orthodox claim to bear witness).

This position was certainly affirmed by the highly influential Russian theologian, Georges Florovsky. Florovsky also paved the way, however, for full Orthodox participation in the ecumenical movement by arguing in the 1930s that "it is impossible to state or discern the true limits of the church simply by canonical marks or signs."[14] Florovsky accepted the premise of St. Cyprian that the sacraments are accomplished only in the church, but Cyprian defined "in" too narrowly. After all, the Orthodox have customarily received members from other churches without requiring them to be re-baptized, and in some cases receive ministers without re-ordination—a recognition that the rites performed over them were "valid." "But," wrote Florovsky, "if the sacraments are

---

[12]In Kinnamon and Cope, 20, 21.
[13]In Kinnamon and Cope, 92.
[14]In Kinnamon and Cope, 84.

performed, it can only be by virtue of the Holy Spirit." And it is the presence of the Spirit, not canonical restrictions, that defines the real boundaries of the church.

This insight found its way into what is known as the Toronto Statement (1950), the World Council's most extensive and authoritative attempt at self-definition: "The member churches recognize that the membership of the Church of Christ is more inclusive than the membership of their own church body."[15] Members may not yet accept each other as "true and pure churches," but they do affirm that God has bound them in Christ to sisters and brothers beyond their own community of faith.

According to theologian Jean Tillard, it was a similar awareness of "the church outside the canonical limits" that changed the ecumenical orientation of Roman Catholic bishops during the Second Vatican Council.

> The discovery that a real holy life, sometimes leading to martyrdom, was existing outside the canonical borders of the Catholic Church, the awareness that the teaching of the gospel was faithfully kept in communities not in communion with the Roman *magisterium,* the experience that the activities of ministers in many of these groups were in harmony with what the Catholic tradition sees as the task of the *episcope*–all of this obliged Catholic theologians to recognize that there the Holy Spirit was at work.[16]

The documents of Vatican II thus affirm that, while the one church "subsists in" the Roman Catholic Church, there are elements of church beyond its visible boundaries.

The entry of the Catholic Church into the ecumenical movement was also greatly helped by the insistence of Cardinal Augustin Bea that baptism is the sign of our given unity in Christ. The "Decree on Ecumenism" from Vatican II puts it this way: "Men [and women] who believe in Christ and have been properly baptized are brought into certain, though imperfect, communion with the Catholic Church." They have been incorporated into Christ, marked by the Spirit, and must be "accepted as brothers [and sisters] by the children of the

---

[15]In Kinnamon and Cope, 466.

[16]J. M. R. Tillard, "The Roman Catholic Church and Ecumenism," in *The Vision of Christian Unity,* ed. Thomas F. Best and Theodore J. Nottingham (Indianapolis: Oikoumene Publications, 1997), 191–92.

Catholic Church."[17] This has been strongly reiterated by Pope John Paul II, who—in his 1995 encyclical *On Commitment to Ecumenism (Ut Unum Sint)*—speaks of "the deep communion, linked to the baptismal character, which the Spirit fosters in spite of historical and canonical divisions."[18]

The idea of "given unity" has actually been harder for many Protestants, especially so-called evangelical and free church Protestants, to accept because they think of the church as a voluntary association of believers whose decisions give shape to the community. Free church Protestants may well understand themselves to be spiritually related to other believers in invisible fellowship, but the visible unity *of the church* is a secondary concern. This position is exacerbated in the United States, and all places where it has influence, by the climate of the culture. "Our ontological individualism," writes sociologist Robert Bellah, "finds it hard to comprehend the social realism of the church— the idea that the church is prior to individuals and not just the product of them."[19] Christians shaped by such a sociological context often find it difficult to take seriously either the church's given unity or the divisions that obscure it. They may well respond to a call for cooperation, but without real understanding of what it means to say that God has bound us to one another in Christ prior to any decisions we make about it.

* * *

The predominance of this view may be one of the reasons why we now see far less emphasis in ecumenical literature on God's given unity than on the efforts of the churches to relate to one another. The most globally influential statement on unity of the past two decades is "The Unity of the Church as Koinonia: Gift and Calling," approved by the Seventh Assembly of the WCC (Canberra, 1991).[20] (See appendix 10 for this document.) Despite its title, there is no reference in the actual text to "the Christian *koinonia* which already exists among the separated churches" (Outler). Rather, the emphasis is on the calling of these churches to "draw close to one another" through acts of mutual recognition and common witness. The Holy Spirit figures prominently as the one who comforts and disturbs us throughout "the process of praying, working and struggling for unity," but that is hardly the same

---

[17] In Kinnamon and Cope, 29.

[18] John Paul II, *On Commitment to Ecumenism*, para. 42.

[19] Robert N. Bellah et al., *Habits of the Heart: Individualism and Commitment in American Life* (New York: Harper and Row, 1985), 244.

[20] In Kinnamon and Cope, 124–25.

as Temple's claim that "because [the Spirit] is one, those in whom he is active are one fellowship in him."

In a book published just prior to the Canberra Assembly, Konrad Raiser, the present general secretary of the WCC, observes that

> The starting point [in ecumenical conversations] is no longer the unity given us in Christ as "God's gift and our task" which must be made visible and real, but the actually existing differences [between the churches]...The maintenance of the unity and integrity of one's own church has become the supreme aim of church leaders. Thus, reconciliation, balancing the differences between church traditions, is, it must be realistically admitted, the maximum ecumenical unity which can be achieved.[21]

I need to acknowledge that Raiser, while not a fan of this new emphasis on "church politics," also has reservations about the traditional language of given unity—namely, that it may not take seriously enough the experience of actual history. His analysis, however, underscores the shift I am trying to describe.

A prime example, in my judgment, is a statement entitled "Our Ecumenical Vision," prepared for the WCC's eighth assembly (Harare, 1998). (See appendix 11 for this document.) The dominant image is that of a journey that the member churches commit themselves to undertake:

> We are drawn by the vision of a church that will bring all people into communion with God and with one another...[As if the church were the agent of such communion! As if God had not already acted to overcome our estrangement, doing for us what we cannot do for ourselves!] We are challenged by the vision of a church, the people of God on the way together, confronting all divisions of race, gender, age or culture, striving to realize justice and peace, upholding the integrity of creation...Neither failures nor uncertainties, neither fears nor threats, will weaken our intention to continue to walk together on the way to unity, welcoming those who would join us on this journey, widening our common vision, discovering new ways of witnessing and acting together in faith.[22]

---

[21]Konrad Raiser, *Ecumenism in Transition: A Paradigm Shift in the Ecumenical Movement?* trans. Tony Coates (Geneva: WCC, 1991), 75–76.

[22]Diane Kessler, ed., *Together on the Way: Official Report of the Eighth Assembly of the World Council of Churches* (Geneva: WCC, 1999), 113–15.

There is no suggestion that this journey is not an option, but an expression of our fundamental identity in Christ.

The statement does give thanks "that the triune God has drawn our churches closer together"–but, again, the starting point is not given unity but present division. The statement also speaks of "Jesus Christ who has called us to be one"–but, again, the focus is on calling rather than gift. As I experienced it, there was little public longing in Harare for visible communion among the churches. Instead, we celebrated the fact that we were there together at all–because, without a conviction that we *are* one body (thanks be to God), anything more seems unlikely, if not impossible, in the face of present conflicts.

Of course, the ecumenical movement *is* hard work. But that's the point. We will not likely continue on this journey–in the face of cultural fragmentation, in the face of liberal-conservative animosities, in the face of political antagonisms–unless we recognize that our oneness in Christ is itself a central truth of the gospel. Of course, there *are* theological differences that must be reconciled if we are to confess Jesus Christ together before the world. But the argument made by Temple and Visser't Hooft is that the hard work of reaching theological consensus is a *consequence* of our fundamental communion in Christ, not a *prerequisite* for it. "God has given to his people in Jesus Christ," said the delegates to the WCC's Amsterdam Assembly, "a unity which is his creation and not our achievement...It is in the light of that unity that we can face our deepest difference [the difference between "catholic" and "protestant" conceptions of church], still loving one another in Christ and walking by faith in him alone."[23]

A powerful expression of this insight was provided by Mennonite scholar John Howard Yoder. The functional meaning or implication of church unity, wrote Yoder,

> is not that people agree and, therefore, work together but that where they disagree they recognize the need to talk together with a view to reconciliation. When that meaning is not recognized and acknowledged, i.e., where people operate on the assumption that unity is the product of agreement, this is the sociological form of works religion, namely the understanding that the reality of the gospel is the product of human

---

[23]"The Universal Church in God's Design," in World Council of Churches, *Man's Disorder and God's Design,* The Amsterdam Assembly Series (New York: Harper, 1948), 204.

performance. This is to deny the gift quality of the gospel, which is precisely that we have been, despite ourselves, made one with people with whom we were not one.[24]

This deserves repeating. The notion that unity is synonymous with, or dependent on, agreement is a form of "works religion"—as if *our* agreement on doctrine or social justice or anything else could constitute the unity of God's church.

This point, it seems to me, is often overlooked in the way churches approach ecumenical dialogue: seeking to negotiate agreements as a prerequisite for communion. But one recent dialogue that got it right, in my judgment, is the "Formula of Agreement" approved by four U.S. churches—the Evangelical Lutheran Church in America, the Presbyterian Church (USA), the Reformed Church in America, and the United Church of Christ—in 1997. As the final report of the dialogue committee puts it, ecumenical conversations generally proceed according to a conditional logic: "if...then." If certain conditions are met, then certain steps can be taken toward one another. Instead, they propose a logic of "because...therefore."[25] This, of course, is the logic of the gospel: Not, if we love our neighbor, then God will love us; but, because God loves us, therefore we are freed and empowered to love our neighbor. In the same way, the logic of the ecumenical movement is not if we agree, then we can be one in Christ. Rather, because we are one in Christ, therefore we are freed and empowered to seek common mind on those matters that have kept us apart.

* * *

We come now to the bottom line: This first element of the ecumenical vision—that Christians, while not yet living the unity for which Christ prayed, are already one through the gracious initiative of God—is both what gives the ecumenical movement its prophetic edge and what raises its most difficult challenge. To put it in terms of contemporary headlines, Christians in the United States are related by blood to Christians in Iraq and Yugoslavia; it is a sinful denial of our very identity to say, "We have no need of you" or "You have no claim on us." The defining event for ecumenists in the first half of the last century

<hr/>

[24]John Howard Yoder, *The Royal Priesthood: Essays Ecclesiological and Ecumenical* (Grand Rapids, Mich.: Eerdmans, 1994), 292.

[25]Keith F. Nickle and Timothy F. Lull, *A Common Calling: The Report of the Lutheran-Reform Committee for Theological Conversations, 1988–1992* (Minneapolis: Augsburg Press, 1993), 57.

was most certainly World War II. Delegates to the World Conference on Life and Work held in Oxford in the summer of 1937 agreed that "if war breaks out, then pre-eminently the church must manifestly be the church, still united as the one body of Christ, though the nations wherein it is planted fight each other"[26]–a sentence that, as Visser't Hooft noted, "was to become a charter for the ecumenical movement in the Second World War."[27]

The history of the movement is filled with images of fellowship in the midst of political, social, and military conflict: the evident solidarity between Japanese and Chinese delegations at the 1938 meeting of the International Missionary Council, the rapport in WCC settings during the Cold War era between Christians from western Europe and those from the Soviet bloc, the embrace of leaders from the China Christian Council and the Presbyterian Church in Taiwan at the WCC Assembly in Canberra... It was in Canberra in February of 1991, while American bombs rained down on Iraq, that I met the Chaldean Catholic Bishop of Baghdad and heard him say, "These bombs are also falling on you"– a profound lesson for me in ecumenical ecclesiology.

I once asked Emilio Castro, the WCC's fourth general secretary, what one moment best captured for him the vision of the ecumenical movement. He recalled a discussion on the meaning of Christian fellowship at a meeting of the Council's Central Committee in 1972. One of the speakers was General T. B. Simatupang, a leader in Indonesia's struggle for independence from the Netherlands. "Nothing on earth," Castro remembers him saying, "can unite me with the Dutch. But in Jesus Christ we are one."

Many Christians, however, including many involved in the ecumenical movement, find such a statement not only difficult but offensive. They may well reject the idea that unity is possible only with those who share their "fundamentals" of the faith, while yet insisting that unity is possible only with those who share a particular social-political struggle. A "given unity" of all who confess Christ is unthinkable for them because it would mean that they were bound in I-can't-say-I-have-no-need-of-you fellowship with persons they regard as oppressors.

But isn't this the message of scripture? "I find," said Eivind Berggrav to a meeting of the WCC's Central Committee at the height of the Cold

---

[26]Quoted in W. A. Visser't Hooft, *Memoirs* (London: SCM Press, 1973), 73.
[27]Visser't Hooft, *Memoirs*, 73.

War, "that the New Testament demands of me that I shall be willing to accept as a full brother in Christ a man who seems to me perhaps quite dangerous in his political or economic views."[28] And isn't this the vision of the ecumenical movement? If I understand it correctly, the movement has consistently maintained, through assembly reports and the statements of its leaders, that our shared identity as Christians should take precedence over all other labels and loyalties. We are black *Christians* and white *Christians* and are, therefore, related at a level deeper than race. We are U.S. Christians and Cuban Christians and are, therefore, related at a level deeper than nationality. We are Protestant Christians and Catholic Christians and are, therefore, related at a level deeper than church tradition. We are liberal Christians and conservative Christians and are, therefore, related at a level deeper than ideology. We are pro-life Christians and pro-choice Christians and are, therefore, related at a level deeper even than such convictions.

Ecumenism is not defined by adherence to a particular agenda but by affirmation of a particular vision that insists that God has fashioned the church as a single people, even when the agenda of its members conflict. And *precisely for that reason,* the movement has stood firmly against all that divides what God has put together.

Perhaps the most profound (if overlooked) discussion of this challenge is a short document, "Towards Unity in Tension," written by the WCC's Faith and Order Commission at its 1974 meeting in Accra, Ghana. (See appendix 9 for this document.) The tone is appropriately paradoxical. The report acknowledges that "Christians involved in the struggle for liberation in fact often find themselves closer to others who share the struggle with them, Christian or not, than to other Christians who are not committed to it."[29] Further, any church unity that hinders the struggle for justice and freedom would be oppressive, and any "easy" unity that papers over fundamental differences would be empty, false.

At the same time, we may believe in and give witness to our unity in Christ, even with those from whom we may, for his sake, have to part. Christian faith trusts in the reality of grace in which it is empowered to bear the tensions of conflicts. Jesus Christ accepted the necessity of conflict, yet transcended it in his death on the cross. He took upon himself the cost of conflict; forces of division are finally overcome in the unity

---

[28]Quoted in Visser't Hooft, *Memoirs*, 225.
[29]In Kinnamon and Cope, 109.

that Christ creates and gives, as he leads all things to unity in himself. The church has also been given remarkable anticipations of this unity, even in the midst of severe conflict. The church must, therefore, bear the tension of conflicts within itself, and so fulfil its ministry of reconciliation in obedience to the Lord, who chooses to sacrifice himself rather than to confer on the forces of division any ultimate authority.[30]

Tom Best, long-time member of the WCC staff, has referred to this as the "Accra Principle": "the need for acceptance and continuing dialogue between representatives of differing positions, churches and traditions, in the face even of serious differences of belief and practice." The crucial theological premise behind this principle, writes Best, is that "unity is not something which we have to create, but is a reality given already by God."[31]

I love the way that this vision of church is expressed in the writings of Elizabeth Templeton, a Scottish Reformed theologian who is a frequent speaker at ecumenical conferences. The following paragraph is from her book *The Strangeness of God:*

> [The Church] must refuse to domesticate our exclusions as having a part in God's future. In this it challenges all the belongings which define us *against* one another. So help him God, Gerry Adams is called to banquet with Ian Paisley. So help me God, I am called to banquet with both, and everything in my guts doesn't want to! I must, where I humanly belong, take sides on issues involving both. Yet I am only allowed to take sides on the basis of a recognition that who I am in Christ in some sense has to take them in.[32]

Templeton emphasizes the future reign of God in which our exclusions will have no place, but God's gift of unity is still the bottom line. There *are* times when Christians must take sides against sisters and brothers in the church. But even in such moments, our understanding of church must be shaped more by theology than by politics. Even in such moments, we must recognize that the "them" we oppose are, in some fundamental way, "us." The ecumenical church cannot fear controversy or confrontation, for that is paralyzing, but it must hate division because the story by which we live tells us that we have been

---

[30]Ibid.

[31]Thomas F. Best, ed., *Beyond Unity-in-Tension* (Geneva: WCC, 1988), 31.

[32]Elizabeth Templeton, *The Strangeness of God* (London: Arthur James, 1993), 94.

linked in communion with persons we otherwise would shun. Nothing else can testify so powerfully that our trust is in God, not in the things or even the communities of our devising.

*   *   *

Templeton was a speaker at the Fifth World Conference on Faith and Order (Santiago de Compostela, Spain, 1993), where she contended that a new fault-line runs through the middle of the ecumenical movement.

> This fault-line has on the one side people who believe that, whatever disputes remain about doctrine, order, praxis, they are trivial in the light of the confidence that we *are* one in Christ, and that we could and should be already exploring that confidence in sacramental life, exchangeable ministry and common service. On the other side are those who find it mere pious or sentimental fiction that we are all one, until we can wrestle into concrete agreed articulation what we believe, how we structure our discipline and liturgical life, and sanction our practice in the light of God's self-disclosure.[33]

As I see it, the "classic" ecumenical vision says both yes and no to both sides of this divide. Yes, we are already one; but no, this does not mean that we should minimize the significance of our differences regarding doctrinal truth and mission faithfulness. Rather, it is the recognition of how God has bound us in one body that provides the proper setting for the work we undertake through the ecumenical movement. The burden of proof is on those who would justify separateness. And leaving the table is simply not an option.

---

[33]Elizabeth Templeton, "Towards the Realization of Common Life," in *On the Way to Fuller Koinonia: Official Report of the Fifth World Conference on Faith and Order,* ed. Thomas F. Best and Günther Gassmann (Geneva: WCC, 1994), 120.

2

Unity and Renewal

Why Cooperation Is Not the Goal of Ecumenism

Renewal of the church has been at the top of the ecumenical agenda, inseparable from unity, almost from the beginning of the modern ecumenical movement. Faith and Order and Life and Work (see appendix 1 for information on these streams of ecumenism) had different recipes for how renewal happens—one emphasizing a new commitment to shared service, the other a common recovery of the full apostolic faith—but both spoke explicitly of renewal in their early conferences. For example, the unofficial slogan of the Oxford conference on Life and Work (1937)—"Let the church be the church"—was understood as a call for radical renewal, a call for the church not to be conformed to the world. Meanwhile, the struggle of the Confessing Church in Germany, so crucial to the formation of the ecumenical vision, underscored that the unity we seek is not unity at any price. A joining of churches that are fundamentally disobedient to the gospel is hardly the goal.

This emphasis on renewal was naturally carried into the World Council of Churches, whose first assembly (Amsterdam, 1948) met under the theme, "Man's Disorder and God's Design." The "call to the churches" to participate in this historic event put the matter bluntly:

"We have failed because we ourselves have been partakers in [humanity's] disorder. Our first and deepest need is not new organization, but the renewal, or rather the rebirth of the actual churches."[1] This idea was echoed thirteen years later at the Council's third assembly in New Delhi: "The achievement of unity will involve nothing less than the death and re-birth of many forms of church life as we have known them...nothing less costly can finally suffice."[2] The very theme of the fourth assembly (Uppsala, 1968) was "Behold, I make all things new."

The clearest statement of the vision again comes from Willem Visser't Hooft. "The theme of the ecumenical movement," he wrote in *The Pressure of Our Common Calling*, "is not unity as an isolated goal; it is unity as the outcome of the common effort to express the integrity and wholeness of the church of Christ. It is unity through renewal."[3] This conviction was the focus of Visser't Hooft's 1955 Dale Lectures at Oxford University, subsequently published as *The Renewal of the Church*. There he pointed out that in the history of the church, those who emphasize church unity have often looked with suspicion on efforts at renewal and the disruption they inevitably create, while those who emphasize renewal of Christian life have often viewed the language of church unity as a cover for preservation of the status quo.[4] The genius of the modern ecumenical movement is precisely its insistence that this is a false opposition.

Visser't Hooft argued, on the basis of scripture, that unity and renewal help define each other. Ezekiel prophesies, and the dry bones (a figure for "the whole house of Israel") come together, but such "unity" is meaningless until the breath of God gives them life (Ezekiel 37:1–14). In Romans 12, Paul admonishes his sisters and bothers in Christ to be "transformed by the renewing of your minds," and makes that call specific by immediately speaking of the one body whose many members share their diverse spiritual gifts for the common good.

As I suggested in the Introduction, one of the most insightful books ever written on the ecumenical movement is *And Yet It Moves* by one-time WCC staff member, Ernst Lange. Since the Council's Amsterdam Assembly, wrote Lange in the 1970s,

---

[1]Quoted in W. A. Visser't Hooft, *The Renewal of the Church* (London: SCM Press, 1956), 123.

[2]Michael Kinnamon and Brian E. Cope, eds., *The Ecumenical Movement: An Anthology of Key Texts and Voices* (Geneva: WCC; Grand Rapids, Mich.: Eerdmans, 1997), 89.

[3]W. A. Visser't Hooft, *The Pressure of Our Common Calling* (Garden City, N.Y.: Doubleday, 1959), 27.

[4]Visser't Hooft, *Renewal,* chap. 7.

The indissoluble connection between "unity" and "renewal" has been one of the constant formulas of ecumenical theory and practice. Unity can only come through the renewal of the "actual churches." Yet at the same time, unity is itself an ecumenical way to renewal. As the churches are radically renewed, they unite. As they seek unity on the basis of the fundamentals of faith, they are renewed.[5]

Lange observed that there has been frequent controversy over the means to and meaning of renewal. Does renewal come through change, through the search for new forms of church appropriate to mission in a changing world, or through continuity, through a recovery of the full apostolic witness? There has generally been little controversy, however, over the linkage of these concepts in the ecumenical vision. The unity we seek is not simply a mutual acceptance of what we now are, but a "common quest for the renewed obedience of the one church of Jesus Christ in its faith, its life, its mission and its compassionate response to the world's anguish."[6] To put it plainly, a renewal movement that does not seek to overcome barriers between followers of Christ is not truly "ecumenical," just as a unity movement that does not seek to renew our common life through closer identification with our Lord does not deserve the label.

Thus, I am worried by indications that the theme of unity-through-renewal is less prominent in the movement's contemporary literature. For example, the vision statement from the WCC's 1998 Harare Assembly, referred to in chapter 1, never uses the language of renewal. The ideas of new mission and new community are implicitly present, but the themes are not related, are left as discrete items on a list of longings—and this is surely an impoverishment.

* * *

I want to come at this from another direction in order to identify more clearly the problem that, as I see it, is sapping the vitality of this modern reformation. The basic insight is deceptively simple: The church is renewed through the sharing of gifts that is possible once we recognize our given unity. When churches live in isolation, their

---

[5]Ernst Lange, *And Yet It Moves: Dream and Reality of the Ecumenical Movement,* trans. Edwin Robertson (Grand Rapids, Mich.: Eerdmans, 1997), 107.

[6]David M. Gill, "Whom God Hath Joined Together: Churches and Councils of Churches," *The Ecumenical Review* 42 (January 1991): 46.

theological gene pools get depleted! According to the Toronto Statement, produced by the WCC's Central Committee in 1950, a basic assumption behind the Council is that "the member churches enter into spiritual relationships through which they seek to learn from each other and to give help to each other in order that the body of Christ may be built up and that the life of the churches may be renewed"[7]–a point repeated by nearly every early leader of the movement. By the end of the 1960s, this understanding of shared gifts was extended beyond the gifts entrusted to confessional traditions to include a sharing among cultures. The following is from the WCC's Nairobi Assembly (1975):

> We have found this confession of Christ out of our various cultural contexts to be not only a mutually inspiring, but also a mutually corrective exchange. Without this sharing our individual affirmations would gradually become poorer and narrower. We need each other to regain the lost dimensions of confessing Christ and to discover dimensions unknown to us before. Sharing in this way, we are all changed and our cultures are transformed.[8]

The whole emphasis in 1 Corinthians 12, noted Visser't Hooft, is on humble receptivity. The danger is not that members of the body will say, "You have no need of me," but that they will say, "I have no need of you." The most unecumenical statement in all of scripture is that attributed in Revelation to the church at Laodicea: "I am rich, I have prospered, and I need nothing" (3:17).[9]

Unfortunately, while this insight is often affirmed in principle, it is widely violated in practice. The great New Testament scholar and ecumenist Raymond Brown once observed that Christians generally read scripture to assure themselves that they are right rather than to discover where they haven't been listening[10]–and the same, it seems to me, can be said about much ecumenical dialogue. To take only one prominent example, the forty-page official response of the Roman Catholic Church to the famous Faith and Order text *Baptism, Eucharist, and Ministry* (BEM) never suggests that Catholics have anything new

---

[7]In Kinnamon and Cope, 468.

[8]David M. Paton, ed., *Breaking Barriers: The Official Report of the Fifth Assembly of the World Council of Churches* (London: SPCK, 1976), 46.

[9]Visser't Hooft, *Pressure*, 72.

[10]Raymond E. Brown, *The Churches the Apostles Left Behind* (New York: Paulist Press, 1984), 150.

to learn from this dialogue involving leading Protestant, Orthodox, and Catholic theologians from six continents. The response acknowledges that a study of BEM can be "an enriching experience," but the entire focus is on whether the text conforms to historic Catholic teaching.[11]

By way of contrast, the relationship of full communion involving the Evangelical Lutheran Church in America and three U.S. Reformed churches (mentioned in chapter 1) is based on the principle of "mutual affirmation and admonition." The following passage is typical of the dialogue committee's report:

> When Lutherans finalize and repristinate the theology of the sixteenth century, they need the corrective witness of the Reformed tradition concerning the continuing need for reformation and a fresh appropriation of the church's faith. When Reformed Christians overemphasize primacy of the contemporary situation, they need the corrective witness of the Lutheran focus on the authority of the ecumenical creeds and the Reformation confessions.[12]

* * *

This language of renewal through the sharing of gifts, like that of given unity, creates some difficulty for the Orthodox. All Christians recognize a distinction between the *una sancta,* the eternal church that needs no renewal, and the historical church that stands everywhere and always in need of it. Tom Best nicely summarizes the tension caused by such definitional ambiguity.

> Those who understand the church primarily in terms of its eternal reality will inevitably feel that others, with their readiness to speak of "change" and "renewal," are compromising the "ontological dignity" of the church; those who, from another perspective, speak of reform or growth in the life of the church will feel blocked by a refusal to take seriously the historical, institutional aspects of the church, or the reality of human sinfulness.[13]

---

[11]Max Thurian, ed., *Churches Respond to BEM,* vol. 6 (Geneva: WCC, 1988), 1–40.
[12]Keith F. Nickle and Timothy F. Lull, *A Common Calling: The Report of the Lutheran-Reform Committee for Theological Conversations, 1988–1992* (Minneapolis: Augsburg, 1993), 30.
[13]Thomas F. Best, ed., *Beyond Unity-in-Tension* (Geneva: WCC, 1988), 19.

Orthodox ecclesiology emphasizes that the church is marked by intrinsic newness and perfection because of its identification with the reality of Christ. Most Orthodox leaders involved in the ecumenical movement acknowledge, however, that the church is also scarred by the sinfulness of its members (not that the church sins but that there is sin in the church) and, therefore, needs a more complete realization of the gospel in its earthly, institutional life. Thus, on the occasion of the WCC's twenty-fifth anniversary, the Ecumenical Patriarch acknowledged that the Orthodox have been enriched by the encounter with Western church life and theology as well as by material assistance. "These have all helped to build up Christ in the hearts of millions of distressed Christians and their fellow sufferers."[14]

To take a more specific example, the Orthodox Theological Society, in its response to BEM, gave thanks for the way the text forces Orthodox Christians to examine current practices. They cited, for example, the paragraph that warns against "indiscriminate baptism" of infants. "The criticism is valid. There are many instances when we Orthodox baptize children where there is little or no conscious resolve on the part of the parents or sponsors to raise that child 'to a mature commitment to Christ.'"[15] Orthodox theologians involved in the movement, such as Greek scholar Nikos Nissiotis, speak of how "the Orthodox have to test their ecclesiocentric, liturgical-eucharistic understanding of history within the fellowship of the WCC and check whether this kind of emphasis in their theology is not tempting them to neglect the historical and concrete tasks of the church as such in the modern world." Ecumenism, argued Nissiotis, is a "mutual correction of traditions."[16]

The Roman Catholic Church, despite my earlier criticism of its official response to BEM, has publicly and frequently linked renewal and unity in its statements on ecumenism. It was the concern for renewal that helped lead the Catholic Church to embrace ecumenism at Vatican II. (*Aggiornamento*, the term often used by Pope John XXIII to clarify his hopes for the Council, means "bringing up to date.") And Pope John Paul II made the connection explicit in his 1995 encyclical *Ut Unum Sint*:

---

[14]"Declaration of the Ecumenical Patriarch on the Occasion of the 25th Anniversary of the World Council of Churches," *The Ecumenical Review* 25 (October 1973): 477.

[15]Mimeographed report of the 1983 meeting of the Orthodox Theological Society in America.

[16]Quoted in Martin Conway, *Journeying Together towards Jubilee* (privately published, 1999), 21.

Thanks to ecumenism, our contemplation of "the mighty works of God" has been enriched by new horizons...By engaging in frank dialogue, communities help one another to look at themselves together in light of the apostolic Tradition. This leads them to ask themselves whether they truly express in an adequate way all that the Holy Spirit has transmitted through the apostles.[17]

The breakthrough of the past generation, wrote Jean Tillard, a leading figure in Catholic ecumenical dialogue during the last quarter of the twentieth century, flowed from the recognition that other churches have gifts to offer that Catholics need to receive.

For instance, the fashion in which the Word of God had been kept and proclaimed in Lutheran churches was challenging the way the Bible was neglected in many Catholic circles...and the tone of the Anglican association of lay persons in the discussion of the central affairs of the church inspired Catholic theologians and church leaders who were struggling with the clericalism which was too much at home in Catholic practice.[18]

Protestants have, of course, regarded reform or renewal as a decisive mark of the church; but, once again, the greatest threat to the ecumenical vision, in my judgment, comes from Protestants, especially Protestants in Europe and North America, who tend to equate "being ecumenical" with tolerant cooperation. Patrick Henry, director of an ecumenical institute in Minnesota, named the problem clearly.

One of the peculiarities of the situation in the United States is that ecumenism has never taken deep root. There has been wide-spread, even sustained, interdenominationalism; but the challenge of genuine ecumenism—...a challenge that brings institutional prerogatives to judgment—has been muted by the undeniable success of denominations and their efforts to work together. The great new fact of our era [William Temple's description of the ecumenical movement] has been transformed, in the United States, into an illustration of the general, and

---

[17]John Paul II, *On Commitment to Ecumenism,* paras. 15, 16.
[18]J. M. R. Tillard, "The Roman Catholic Church and Ecumenism," in *The Vision of Christian Unity,* ed. Thomas F. Best and Theodore J. Nottingham (Indianapolis: Oikoumene Publications, 1997), 192.

generally laudable, American capacity for joint effort to achieve agreed-on goals.[19]

This isn't to say that church life isn't changing. Denominational boundaries are becoming very porous; most mainline Protestants, I suspect, now find Reformation-era disputes quaintly irrelevant. But this is ecumenism by erosion, not by mutual enrichment—and it will not renew us.

A fine example of ecumenism, I am sometimes told, is Habitat for Humanity. My wife and I are strong supporters of Habitat; she was for several years a member of its board of directors. But Habitat for Humanity is an example of interdenominational—or even interfaith—cooperation, not ecumenism as understood by the movement's pioneers. I want to suggest four points of contrast:

1. Cooperative activity is the result of human decision. Ecumenical commitment, we confess, is the result of a divine gift of community. We can decide whether or not to cooperate—and, humanly speaking, there may sometimes be good reasons not to do so. But if we would be Christ's disciples, then, theologically speaking, we don't have a choice whether or not to seek unity with others who also are in him. Cooperation is based on the need or desire to accomplish some end. Ecumenical commitment is based on a theological imperative. Yes, our unity is so "that the world may believe" (John 17:21), but it is also an end in itself. To live as one reconciled fellowship is to be what we are, whether or not we can perceive any practical benefits from it.

2. Since the aim of cooperative activity is the achievement of a particular, immediate purpose, such activity is, by its very nature, short-lived. The goal of ecumenical commitment, by way of contrast, is the realization of comprehensive long-term community. Ecumenical engagement should be anything but short-term.

3. Cooperation aimed, for example, at building houses is usually undermined when other concerns are introduced into the picture. A concern to grow in common understanding of baptism would likely sink a Habitat project. An aggressive justice agenda can scuttle efforts at cooperative service. Ecumenism, however, lives deliberately with tensions—unity *and* justice, freedom *and* reconciliation—that advocates of cooperative ventures seek to avoid.

---

[19]Patrick G. Henry, "From Breakthrough to Breakthrough," *The Ecumenical Review* 42 (January 1991): 23.

Similarly, cooperation is usually more successful when differences are ignored or when the groups or persons involved are relatively like-minded. By contrast, the ecumenical vision of unity through the sharing of *diverse* gifts (discussed more fully in chapter 4) must sometimes forsake cooperative efficiency for the hard work of living intentionally through disagreement. Indeed, since it is God's unity that we seek to make visible, ecumenical commitment may require Christians to disrupt our partial, temporary unities for the sake of more authentic fellowship.

4. Most importantly, churches can cooperate without being changed, and the cooperation of unrenewed churches is, quite simply, not the ecumenical goal. The point is not that Christians ought to get along, but that Christians need one another and are given one another in order to be the church. The ecumenical confession is that apart from one another we are impoverished. Visser't Hooft put it this way in *The Pressure of Our Common Calling:*

> Cooperation is not unity. A consensus about social action combined with a moratorium on theological and doctrinal discussion leads easily to the conclusion that the churches have done enough when they have established cooperative relationships. But this is a false conclusion for unity in Christ is unity in the deepest convictions and unity which embraces all of life. Those who accept cooperation as sufficient are in danger of retarding the growth of that true unity.[20]

This discussion needs to be nuanced. Cooperation can be an important stage on the way toward deeper unity. (Ecumenical primers sometimes speak of five stages of interchurch relations: competition, coexistence, cooperation, commitment, and communion.) Acting together may help draw churches into closer, more committed relationship. They should do all things together that are now possible in anticipation of the day when they can be together in fuller fellowship. Beyond that, cooperation is also a natural expression of Christian unity. Those who know themselves to be one in Christ will surely work together to build houses or help the poor. The ecumenical vision is impoverished, however, when cooperation is seen as a sufficient expression of, or alternative to, communion. If seen as an end in itself, cooperation actually reinforces the status quo and, thus, undercuts the impulse for renewal.

---

[20]Visser't Hooft, *Pressure,* 18.

* * *

I want to shift the discussion slightly in order to reinforce the danger of contemporary impoverishment. Christians, of course, may agree that unity is a gift to be made visible and still disagree on what it would mean to be visibly one. The Toronto Statement acknowledged that "membership in the World Council does not imply the acceptance of a specific doctrine concerning the nature of church unity."[21] After all, the various confessional traditions brought with them into the ecumenical movement different notions of what unity would require. And, beyond that, *models* of unity are, at least to some extent, historically and culturally contextual. Forms of visible unity that make sense in a situation of political monarchy may seem false in a democratic context. Models of unity appropriate to a "modern" society may feel constrictive or cumbersome in the emerging "post-modern" culture.

A favorite model from mid-century until 1970 was "organic union," understood as the structural consolidation of previous denominations. Organically united churches, such as the Church of South India and the United Church of Christ (U.S.), are marked by common patterns of worship, a shared confession of faith, and a structure for making decisions together. The heritages of the previous churches may be honored, but former confessional labels (e.g., Reformed, Methodist, Congregational) are subordinated in favor of a new united identity.

I give thanks for these unions. Millions of Christians today live beyond isolating barriers of the past as a result of these ecumenical ventures. At the same time, it must be acknowledged that real criticism has been leveled against this model: Legitimate gifts of the Spirit, embedded in the denominational heritages, can be lost or overlooked. The focus on structural union can detract from needed emphasis on mission. Resistance to the new united church can lead to new divisions in the body of Christ.

Concerns of this sort helped fuel interest in another model, often called "unity in reconciled diversity." Proponents still speak of a mutual recognition of members and ministers, of eucharist sharing, of common prayer and service, and of some form of joint decision making. The difference, however, is made explicit in a paper produced in 1974 by representatives of the Christian World Communions (e.g., the World Alliance of Reformed Churches and the Lutheran World Federation):

---

[21]In Kinnamon and Cope, 465.

"We consider the variety of denominational heritages legitimate insofar as the truth of the one faith explicates itself in history in a variety of expressions."[22] A single ecclesiastical structure does not insure that division and lovelessness are overcome, even as a plurality of structures and names need not deny the presence of genuine communion. Through dialogue and shared life, the denominations can lose their exclusive character while still continuing as distinctive churches.

Not all ecumenists are persuaded! Lesslie Newbigin, for example, argued that such a proposal is little more than a smoke screen for preserving the status quo, because "it offers an invitation to reunion without repentance and without renewal, to a unity in which we are faced with no searching challenge to our existing faith and practice, but can remain as we are."[23] The wind, however, had clearly shifted direction. Since the early 1970s, there have been very few organic unions, involving churches from different confessional traditions, anywhere in the world. The preferred model is to initiate covenants or full communion relationships among churches that maintain their own structures, traditions, forms of worship, systems of ministerial selection, and mission programs.

The Consultation on Church Union (COCU), a church unity effort involving nine U.S. denominations, is a case study of the shift in models outlined above. Church representatives in COCU set forth a "Plan of Union," calling for one organically united church body, in 1970; but it was rejected by the churches. A new proposal, sent to the churches in 1988, called for them to "commit themselves, before God and each other, to live henceforth in one *covenantal communion* even though they continue to exist in distinct ecclesiastical systems."[24] Elements of covenant communion included mutual recognization of each other as churches (or, better, as parts of the one church of Jesus Christ), mutual recognition that each confesses the same apostolic faith, mutual recognition of members in one baptism, regular celebration of the eucharist together, shared mission (at least on occasion), and the mutual recognition and reconciliation of ordained ministry. Ministry, however, has continued to be problematic; and so a revised proposal asked the churches to bracket the question of ministry, reserving it for later intensive dialogue, while proceeding to inaugurate a new relationship, called Churches Uniting

---

[22]"Reconciled Diversity," *WCC Exchange* (July 1974): 6–9.
[23]Lesslie Newbigin, "All in One Place or All of One Sort?" in *Creation, Christ and Culture*, ed. Richard W. A. McKinney (Edinburgh: T. and T. Clark, 1976), 293.
[24]*Churches in Covenant Communion* (Consultation on Church Union, 1989), 9.

in Christ, marked by the other elements of covenant communion.[25] This proposal has been affirmed by all nine churches, and Churches Uniting in Christ (CUIC) was inaugurated in January 2002.

I am a supporter of Churches Uniting in Christ. Indeed, I have served as COCU's general secretary from 1999 until the inauguration of CUIC. I believe there were understandable reasons not to approve the earlier "Plan of Union," including a legitimate fear on the part of COCU's three predominately African American churches that their distinctive gifts would be swallowed up in a white majority. Had the 1970 "Plan of Union" succeeded, we might have been even less likely to repent, even more likely to glory in our institutional power. Besides, church union should not be thought of as an all-or-nothing, one-time achievement. Testing out different models, through which trust can be built, is surely appropriate, because no one model is a definitive expression of visible unity, a definitive reflection of the gift we have received in Christ.

But there is an obvious danger: namely, that Churches Uniting in Christ, lacking the structural commitment that goes with organic union, will be interpreted minimally rather than maximally. "COCU's plan [of covenant communion]," noted one (sympathetic) observer in a press release, "amounts to laying out a procedure for ecumenical advance without disturbing the inner life of the churches." Staff members of two COCU denominations told me, following the 1988 plenary, that their representatives came back saying, "Don't worry. The proposal we approved [i.e., covenant communion] won't change things here very much, if at all." In the absence of structures for mutual accountability, commitments, however solemnly made, can be ignored.

COCU's theological consensus document strongly underscores the idea of renewal through the sharing of gifts.

> Insofar as Christians have been divided from one another, they have suffered by being deprived of each other's gifts, help, and correction...Each particular church will find, by union with the others, not a loss but expansion of identity, through giving and receiving in a renewed life of faith, worship, fellowship, and ministry.[26]

---

[25]"Recommendation to the Churches," *Mid-Stream* 39 (January–April 2000): ix–xiii.
[26] *The COCU Consensus* (Consultation on Church Union, 1985), 10, 13.

This will only be true, however, if the churches take seriously their covenant with one another.

Models of unity *will* change with historical circumstances. But a unity proposal, if it is to deserve such a label, must be tangible enough and substantive enough to make a witness to the world. It must be intense enough that those in it recognize their responsibility for, and accountability to, one another. It must be costly enough that churches are changed as a result of being in it. And it must be intentional enough that the body of Christ is renewed through the sharing of gifts. To settle for less is surely an impoverishment of the ecumenical vision.

—— 3 ——

Unity and Justice

Why Splitting the Agenda Misses the Point

There is a third absolutely crucial element in what I am calling the ecumenical vision. The unity and renewal of the church (discussed in chapters 1 and 2) are inseparable from and indispensable to the wholeness and renewal of human society—indeed, of all creation. There should be no need to establish that the ecumenical movement has been concerned both with realizing the visible unity of the church—understood as a fully committed fellowship involving such things as shared sacraments, ministry, service, and prayer—and with promoting justice and peace in the wider human community. (A brief history of these themes is found in appendix 1.) What truly distinguishes the ecumenical vision, however, is the insistence that the unity of the church contributes to its mission in the world, even as engagement with the world contributes to the church's unity. This is a movement that, at its best, believes that efforts to confess the gospel together are directly related to overcoming apartheid, a movement that says *Baptism, Eucharist, and Ministry* and Program to Combat Racism in the same breath.

Actually holding such things together, however, has proved extraordinarily difficult. "For some," said the report of the WCC's Vancouver Assembly (1983), the search for a unity in one faith and one eucharistic fellowship seems, at best secondary, at worst irrelevant to the struggles for peace, justice and human dignity; for others, the church's political involvement against the evils of history seems, at best secondary, at worst detrimental to its role as eucharistic community and witness to the gospel.[1]

Even worse, this tendency to split the agenda has frequently been institutionalized in churches and ecumenical organizations. "Justice" and "unity" are relegated to separate departments, setting up a competition for resources and influence. And, to the extent this happens, the vision of the ecumenical movement is, in my judgment, terribly impoverished. Integrating these often-competing priorities has probably been the movement's most persistent and vexing challenge.

It is important to recall that the ecumenical movement began as a series of somewhat discrete initiatives. Three are usually identified when telling the story of modern ecumenism: (1) the Life and Work movement, which sought to foster interchurch aid, to enable common Christian response to the victims of war, poverty, oppression, and natural disaster, and to call the churches to oppose economic and social injustice; (2) the Faith and Order movement, which continues to work at overcoming obstacles to the mutual recognition of members and ministers, at overcoming barriers to shared celebration of the eucharist, at helping the churches to express more fully the apostolic faith, and at discovering ways of making decisions together; and (3) the International Missionary Council, which attempted to promote shared witness and to overcome different understandings and practices of mission and evangelism.

This history of distinctive agendas, and constituencies, built a fragmentation into the movement that has never been fully resolved. But, at least by the 1930s, it was clear to many ecumenical leaders "that ultimately life, work, faith and order are expressions of an existing spiritual unity, and that each requires the other for its complete fruition" (First World Conference on Faith and Order, 1927).[2] Konrad Raiser, current general secretary of the WCC, names some of those leaders while making the same point.

---

[1] David Gill, ed., *Gathered for Life: Official Report of the Sixth Assembly of the World Council of Churches* (Geneva: WCC, 1983), 49.

[2] H. N. Bate, ed., *Faith and Order: Proceedings of the Lausanne World Conference* (Garden City, N.Y.: Doubleday, 1928), 538.

John R. Mott was guided by the goal of the evangelization of the world in this generation; Nathan Söderblom was inspired by the belief in the universal character of the church and sought to establish inter-national friendship through evangelical catholicity; Archbishop Germanos spoke of the need to supplement the emerging League of Nations by a league *(koinonia)* of the churches; and lastly, Bishop Brent envisioned the possibility of achieving unity among the separated churches through careful theological dialogue. The movement did not gain its full momentum, however, until they discovered that these were only different expressions of one integrated vision concerning the calling of the whole church to bring the whole gospel to the whole world.[3]

The primary manifestation of this desired integration is, of course, the World Council of Churches, which began through a union of the Faith and Order and Life and Work movements in 1948 and, by 1961, included the International Missionary Council. Critics have argued that the WCC has been less an integration of these three streams than an institutionalization of their parallel development, but that does not do justice to the repeated attempts to express the essential relationship between, for example, unity and mission or unity and peace. The following statements—first, from the WCC's Central Committee in 1951, and, second, from the Council's second assembly in 1954—are typical of the period.

> [The word *ecumenical*] is properly used to describe everything that relates to the whole task of the whole church to bring the gospel to the whole world. It therefore covers equally the missionary movement and the movement toward unity, and must not be used to describe one in contradistinction to the other.[4]

> We are concerned here with our hopes for the peace and unity of all [hu]mankind, but what greater hope there would be if only our Christian unity were achieved, a unity transcending the ethnic and racial differences of all believers. There is an urgent

---

[3]Konrad Raiser, "Ecumenism in Search of a New Vision," in *The Ecumenical Movement: An Anthology of Key Texts and Voices,* ed. Michael Kinnamon and Brian E. Cope (Geneva: WCC; Grand Rapids, Mich.: Eerdmans, 1997), 71.

[4]In Michael Kinnamon and Brian E. Cope, eds., *The Ecumenical Movement: An Anthology of Key Texts and Voices* (Geneva: WCC; Grand Rapids, Mich.: Eerdmans, 1997), 5.

and immediate task; when it is accomplished how great the further contribution that we might make.[5]

A leading figure in the ecumenical movement, from the founding of the World Council until his death in the 1990s, and a leading advocate for a holistic vision, was Lesslie Newbigin. The following conviction, quoted from Newbigin's book of 1953, *The Household of God,* grew out of his experience with the united Church of South India.

> I do not think that a resolute dealing with our divisions will come except in the context of a quite new acceptance on the part of all the churches of the obligation to bring the gospel to every creature; nor do I think that the world will believe that gospel until it sees more evidence of its power to make us one. These two tasks—mission and unity—must be prosecuted together and in indissoluble relation with one another.[6]

This sentence from his autobiography, *Unfinished Agenda,* is also typical of Newbigin's writings: "There can be for me no escape from the conviction that the essential contribution of the church to peace and justice in the world is a fellowship which actually realizes (even if only in foretaste) that peace and justice which Christ has won for all peoples in his atoning death and resurrection."[7]

This last quotation introduces a key motif of ecumenical literature: the church as a *sign* (and "foretaste") of what God intends for all the world. The 1937 Oxford Conference on Church, Community and State, generally known as the second of the Life and Work conferences, made this point in its eloquent "Message" (see appendix 5):

> The first duty of the church, and its greatest service to the world, is that it be in very deed the church—confessing the true faith, committed to the fulfillment of the will of Christ, its only Lord, and united in Him in a fellowship of love and service...On every side we see men [and women] seeking for a life of fellowship in which they experience their dependence on one another. But because community is sought on the wrong basis, the intensity of the search for it issues in conflict and disintegration. In such a world the church is called to be in its

---

[5] *The Evanston Report: The Second Assembly of the World Council of Churches* (London: SCM Press, 1955), 158.

[6] Lesslie Newbigin, *The Household of God* (New York: Friendship Press, 1954), 174.

[7] Lesslie Newbigin, *Unfinished Agenda* (Grand Rapids, Mich.: Eerdmans, 1985), 253.

own life that fellowship which binds men [and women] together in their common dependence on God and overleaps all barriers of social status, race or nationality.[8]

The delegates at Oxford were, for obvious reasons, acutely aware that the world's "unities" (e.g., Hitler's Reich or the Stalinist state) can be demonic. The church, they were convinced, must show a more excellent way. It was the WCC's fourth assembly (Uppsala, 1968), however, that gave this notion its most famous expression: "The church is bold in speaking of itself as a sign of the coming unity of [hu]mankind"[9]– a line that echoes Vatican II.[10] The church, in other words, doesn't just campaign for peace and justice; it must demonstrate peace and justice in the way its members live with one another. The church doesn't just proclaim Jesus Christ; it must visibly witness to him through the quality of its life as a community.

* * *

The idea of the church's unity as a sign, a demonstration project, has been repeated in numerous ecumenical documents since 1968, but the Uppsala statement was also immediately criticized. Two primary arguments have been offered against it: (1) It seems to claim too much, to be too utopian given the visible brokenness of the church. Yes, the churches may be making headway in their efforts to resolve old disputes over such things as the meaning of baptism. But new breaches are opening between liberals and conservatives, and the denominations continue to be divided by human barriers. As Martin Luther King, Jr., noted, the eleven o'clock hour on Sunday morning is the most segregated hour of the week in the United States. What kind of sign is that?! To claim such a role for the church simply invites ridicule. (2) The statement is too one-directional (Doesn't the world have a few things to teach the church?), or even begins in the wrong place. The report from the Uppsala Assembly sums up what was clearly a growing conviction.

> It seems to many, inside and outside the church, that the struggle for Christian unity in its present form is irrelevant to the immediate crises of our times. The church, they say, should

---

[8]J. H. Oldham, ed., *The Oxford Conference: Official Report* (Chicago: Willett, Clark, 1937), 45, 46–47.

[9]In Kinnamon and Cope, 96.

[10]"Dogmatic Constitution on the Church," para. 1.

seek its unity through solidarity with those forces in modern life, such as the struggle for racial equality, which are drawing men [and women] more closely together, and should give up its concern with patching up its own internal disputes.[11]

One of those voices was Gustavo Gutierrez in his seminal book of 1970, *A Theology of Liberation* (portions of which were first presented at a meeting of a commission jointly sponsored by the Vatican and the WCC).

> Meetings of Christians of different confessions but of the same political opinion are becoming more frequent. This gives rise to ecumenical groups, often marginal to their ecclesiastical authorities, in which Christians share their faith and struggle to create a more just society. The common struggle makes the traditional ecumenical programs seem obsolete ("a marriage between senior citizens" as someone has said) and impels them to look for new paths toward unity.[12]

Ecumenism, according to the previous generation, is primarily a matter of the church getting itself together in order to present the gospel of wholeness to the world. New voices were now contending that it is also a matter (or more a matter) of the church participating in God's mission of wholeness in the world and, thereby, discovering something of its own unity. A paper prepared for the 1967 meeting of the WCC's Faith and Order Commission put the argument unambiguously.

> Church unity is not an end to be pursued for its own sake. Nor is it an object which the church should try to attain as a preparation for more effective mission to the world. The church cannot expect to be fully reconciled to God as a first stage in the restoration of creation, before the world itself, as a second stage, comes to be summed up in Christ...Church unity must be a by-product of the reconciliation of the world. The church can therefore hope for unity to the degree that it directs its efforts outwards, away from its internal concerns and towards the needs of [hu]mankind in general.[13]

---

[11]Norman Goodall, ed., *The Uppsala Report: Official Report of the Fourth Assembly of the World Council of Churches* (Geneva: WCC, 1968), 12.

[12]Gustavo Gutierrez, *A Theology of Liberation*, trans. Caridad Inda and John Eagleson (Maryknoll, N.Y.: Orbis Books, 1973), 104.

[13]*New Directions in Faith and Order: Bristol 1967* (Geneva: WCC, 1968), 139.

The classical schema had been God-church-world (God works through the church in the world). It is time, said a report to Uppsala on the missionary structure of the congregation, that we shifted our thinking to God-world-church. "God's primary relationship is to the world, and it is the world and not the church that is the focus of God's plan."[14]

I find Willem Visser't Hooft's reaction to these developments surprisingly tempered, given his role in the older generation, and very instructive. On the penultimate page of his *Memoirs,* published in 1973, the former general secretary agrees that the churches have indeed begun to think in a different way about the relationship between church and world—less preoccupied with their own life and more concerned with signs of God's reign in the rest of creation. "It seems to me," he concluded,

> that this is not only a perfectly justifiable concern, but also an inevitable consequence of the discoveries which have been made in the history of the [ecumenical] movement. When the World Council gives today such high priority to the issues of world-wide development, or when it takes very concrete steps in the fight against racism, it is certainly not denying the mandate which it has received. When we study the problems of church unity in the light of the unity of [hu]mankind we arc not changing our course altogether, but seeking to bring together two dimensions which have always been there but which had not been sufficiently related to each other.[15]

Many responses, however, have been far less sanguine. One example is that of the well-known German theologian and longtime member of the WCC's Commission on Faith and Order, Wolfhart Pannenberg. The central issue, writes Pannenberg in various articles, is the place of the church in the history of salvation, and it is precisely here that the Uppsala Assembly took a wrong turn. Given the reality of human sinfulness, and the continued presence of worldly powers and principalities, oppression and inequality will not disappear from history—certainly not through human activity. The unity of humankind is, thus, an eschatological concept. The central role of the church, from such a

---

[14] *The Church for Others: A Quest for Structures for Missionary Congregations* (Geneva: WCC, 1967), 16–17.

[15] W. A. Visser't Hooft, *Memoirs* (London: SCM Press, 1973), 367.

perspective, is not to engage in political action aimed at transforming history (which it cannot do and should not create the illusion that it can), but to be the place where persons experience the sacramental presence of the unity of the kingdom that is to come. Whenever the church conceives of itself as an instrument of political change, it becomes perverted and divided by the power of sin at work in the world. The focus of ecumenical work, therefore, should be for the church to become a more convincing, obedient sign of God's promised redemption through its own unity and renewal. It is simply a tragic error to regard the unity of the church as a "by-product" of political struggle, let alone to define church unity in terms of agreement on political issues of the day.[16]

I vividly recall Pannenberg's impassioned argument to this effect at the 1982 meeting of the Faith and Order Commission in Lima, Peru. And I also remember the response from other members of the Commission, especially José Miguez Bonino. The church is not a sign of salvation *alongside* worldly structures, they contended, but a community *within* the world that, through acts of reconciliation and challenge, participates in God's gracious work for all humanity. The church cannot transform society into the kingdom, but it can and must struggle to promote the values of the kingdom—for example, freedom and human dignity—in human community. From this perspective, every part of the church is colored by social-political engagement. We pray and break bread together as those who are involved with the poor and the oppressed.[17]

The past three decades have witnessed repeated attempts to find a credible and compelling common ground. The WCC's Nairobi Assembly (1975) tried to express an integrated vision with its theme, "Jesus Christ Frees *and* Unites"(a theme that I will develop more fully in the Conclusion of this book). The Vancouver Assembly (1983), which celebrated the surprising reception of the text *Baptism, Eucharist and Ministry* (BEM), lifted up a "eucharistic vision" that brings together our "two profoundest ecumenical concerns: the unity and renewal of the church and the healing and destiny of the human community."[18] BEM also points to this integration in passages such as the following:

---

[16]Wolfhart C. Pannenberg, "Unity of the Church–Unity of Humankind: A Critical Appraisal of a Shift in Ecumenical Direction," *Mid-Stream* 21 (October 1982): 485–90.

[17]See Michael Kinnamon, "Insight of the Top: Faith and Order at Lima," *The Ecumenical Review* 34 (April 1982): 138–40.

[18]Gill, 44.

The eucharistic celebration demands reconciliation and sharing among all those regarded as brothers and sisters in the one family of God and is a constant challenge in the search for appropriate relationships in social, economic and political life. All kinds of injustice, racism, separation and lack of freedom are radically challenged when we share in the body and blood of Christ...The Eucharist involves the believer in the central event of the world's history. As participants in the Eucharist, therefore, we prove inconsistent if we are not actively participating in this ongoing restoration of the world's situation and the human condition.[19]

The problem, however, as WCC documents have readily acknowledged, is that these assembly statements "do not go much beyond the affirmation that the various dimensions need to be held together."[20] Ecumenical statements and conciliar structures still give the impression that unity and justice are distinct initiatives. In the United States, Church World Service is now structurally distanced from the National Council of Churches, including its Commission on Faith and Order. The WCC's Harare Assembly (1998), in its vision statement, lists "visible oneness of the body of Christ" and "healing of the human community" as priorities for the Council, but never indicates that they are interdependent—let alone how they are related.

* * *

It is time to make my own position clear. In my judgment, the ecumenical vision is impoverished, not by those who start with justice or by those who start with church unity, but by those who split the agenda, by those who focus on one to the exclusion of the other. The shift from God-church-world to God-world-church should not be minimized, but neither should it be exaggerated. The ecumenical movement can encompass both approaches as long as the basic relationship between church unity and human reconciliation is maintained. Christians acting together for justice, without concern for how this deepens and expands the life of Christian community, are not "ecumenical" in the fullest sense of the word. Just as Christians pursuing sacramental fellowship, without

---

[19]In Kinnamon and Cope, 186 (E 20).
[20]*Towards a Common Understanding and Vision of the World Council of Churches,* (Geneva: WCC, 1993), para. 2.4.

concern for how this deepens and expands their engagement with the world, are not "ecumenical" in the fullest sense of the word.

Since the Uppsala Assembly in 1968, this integration has been a major WCC study theme under several headings: the Unity of the Church and the Unity of Humankind, the Unity of the Church and the Renewal of Human Community, Church and World, and (most recently) Ecclesiology and Ethics. Out of these studies have come a number of convictions that I hope are now widely affirmed:

1. The issues that divide human society (e.g., racism, sexism, economic disparity, violence) also divide the church. Racism, to take one example, is now recognized not only as a question of social justice but as an issue of ecclesiology. Far from being "nontheological," racism signals a radical distortion of the Christian faith and of the church that proclaims it. As obvious as this may sound to twenty-first-century ears, it is a relatively recent insight. An example of this can be seen in the Consultation on Church Union (COCU), a unity effort (referred to in chapter 2) that includes three predominately African American denominations among its nine member churches. Until 1980, COCU's theological consensus document listed racism and sexism as "alerts," issues with "church-dividing potential," in its appendices. Only after that date were such matters incorporated into the main body of the theological text, alongside the more traditional, Reformation-era disputes.

2. Unity and justice, like unity and renewal, help define each other. On the one hand, the search for Christian unity can end up bolstering old forms of domination unless constantly coupled with a commitment to just relationships. The unity we have in Christ is one in which those who have been marginalized find a home. On the other hand, the justice we seek is not merely the coexistence of separated communities, but a community in which walls of hostility have come down. The Church and World study put it this way: "The connection between unity and justice makes it necessary to ask of every expression of visible unity: 'Does it promote justice in the light of the gospel of Jesus Christ both within the church and the world?' And secondly, 'Does it foster the engagement of the church in God's work for justice?'"[21]

3. There are forms of human community, forms of human "unity," that are demonic and must be countered with the vision of God's coming reign (kingdom). Even attempts to realize justice stand under

---

[21] *Church and World: The Unity of the Church and the Renewal of Human Community* (Geneva: WCC, 1990), 49.

judgment of God, whose will—which Christians often discern in such scriptures as Isaiah 65 and Revelation 21—is the measure of all human efforts. A central purpose of the church is to proclaim and embody the promises of God's reign for the world. But the church must do so with humility, because its proclamation, and its efforts at manifesting unity, also are measured by God's future.

4. Like grace, unity is a gift that demands a "costly" response. This idea was raised in chapter 1 in connection with the WCC text "Towards Unity in Tension" (1973). (See appendix 9 for this document.) A more recent treatment of it, however, is the study on Ecclesiology and Ethics. "Cheap unity," according to the study participants, "avoids morally contested issues because they would disturb the unity of the church. Costly unity is discovering that the churches' unity is a gift of pursuing justice and peace."[22] Costly unity may mean an unpopular refusal to endorse the policies of one's nation or ethnic group. It may mean a sacrificial identification with groups despised by the social majority. It does not mean withdrawal from the ambiguities of historical action in order to preserve a shallow harmony within the church.

* * *

No ecumenical leader has defended the integration of unity and justice more eloquently or persistently than M. M. Thomas. When Thomas died in 1996, one Swedish historian wrote that "along with Visser't Hooft, Thomas has had the greatest influence on the modern ecumenical movement"—and I agree with that assessment.

M. M. Thomas was born in 1916 in Kerala, a state on the southwestern coast of India, to a family that was part of the Mar Thoma Church. In the eighteenth century, this ancient tradition, which traces its roots to the apostle Thomas, underwent a reformation initiated by evangelical Anglican missionaries. Thus, the Mar Thoma is sometimes called a "bridge church," combining an eastern liturgical and social life with an evangelical sense of mission. Thomas reflected this heritage in his constant search for synthesis where others saw irreconcilable difference.

In 1968, Thomas was named moderator of the WCC's Central Committee, the first non-Westerner and the only layperson (thus far) to hold that position. His reports and speeches from that period—collected in the book *Towards a Theology of Contemporary Ecumenism*—are

---

[22]Thomas F. Best and Martin Robra, eds., *Ecclesiology and Ethics* (Geneva: WCC, 1997), 6.

brilliant analyses of the movement. They are also, in my reading, examples of "performative speech"—that is, words intended to foster the reality they purportedly describe.

The real revolution of ecumenism in the 1960s, he told the Central Committee in 1973, was the integration of unity, witness, and service. "They have interpenetrated each other so much that church unity, world mission and the struggle for social justice and world community are now seen as impossible to deal with in isolation from each other."[23] Yes, he acknowledged, there is a backlash: old-style advocates of church communion challenging the connection between sacramental fellowship and the unity of humankind, conservative evangelicals growing nervous over the linkage between evangelism and social liberation, ardent defenders of people's liberation opposing any linkage that distracts from the commitment to social revolution. In Thomas's view, however, it is precisely such linkage that makes the church and its theology ecumenical. If the problems of the world are not taken with utmost seriousness, then any unity we Christians achieve regarding doctrine or church order will be shallow and irrelevant. But if the problems of the world *are* taken with such seriousness, then the importance of our given unity should become all the more evident.

The focus of this integration for Thomas is Jesus Christ. In him, God "reveals and realizes" the divine plan, the ultimate destiny, of *all* humanity. In him, *all* things are made new (the theme of the Uppsala Assembly). The resurrection, he wrote, is the good news of a new humanity in which *all* barriers that divide people from one another are or can be overcome. Fellowship in Christ challenges not only denominational separation but also, for example, the barriers of caste that are the particular curse of Indian society. And those who share such fellowship are freed to proclaim this good news through their participation in the social revolutions of their time.[24]

* * *

The first three chapters of this book raise a key underlying question: Is the ecumenical movement best understood as a forum where conflicting perspectives meet in dialogue, or as a renewal effort that boldly declares the gospel's partisanship on behalf of the excluded and

---

[23]M. M. Thomas, "Search for Wholeness and Unity," in Kinnamon and Cope, 44.

[24]See M. M. Thomas, *Towards a Theology of Contemporary Ecumenism* (Madras, India: CLS, 1978), 233, 237, 258.

oppressed? Or, to paraphrase José Miguez Bonino, is the World Council of Churches (and other ecumenical bodies) a "space" where different ecclesial partners get together to celebrate, discuss, and cooperate, or an *avant-garde* movement that challenges the churches through pioneering action and risky theological formulation?[25] The answer, if I understand the movement correctly, is "both." "The world council," wrote Visser't Hooft in 1974, "has a special responsibility to maintain the fellowship between its member churches, for the achievement of this fellowship [with all its tensions] is the real *raison d'etre* of the World Council...But it is a fellowship based on common convictions and called to common witness. An important element in the very substance of our fellowship is what we have hammered out together in our assemblies"[26]—and this includes a common commitment to promote peace with justice, a common commitment to combat racism and sexism, and a shared preferential option for the poor.

Such commitments are not a prerequisite for ecumenical participation; they are part of the fabric of witness now woven through our life together as a result of our common submission to the gospel. I wish the ecumenical movement could speak now with a bolder voice on other questions. But at least there is evidence that a body of shared convictions on difficult issues of our age is emerging thanks to the recognition that we belong together in Christ—if only we can refrain from splitting the agenda.

---

[25]José Miguez Bonino, "The Concern for a Vital and Coherent Theology," *The Ecumenical Review* 41 (April 1989): 172.

[26]W. A. Visser't Hooft, *Has the Ecumenical Movement a Future?* (Belfast, Ireland: Christian Journals Ltd., 1974), 43.

— 4 —

Unity and Diversity

Why Uniting Diversities Is Not the Vision

At the heart of the ecumenical movement is a problem that has troubled political philosophers from Plato to the authors of the United States Constitution: the relationship between the one and the many, between the unity of the community and the diversity of its particular parts. The two concepts—unity and diversity—are symbiotic. "Unity" is meaningful only if it includes in one whole things that are unlike, and "diversity" is only diverse in relation to the other distinctive parts of a whole. So the question is one of emphasis or starting point. Do we say "out of the many, one" *(e pluribus unum)* or "within the one, many"? Do we properly speak of unified diversity or diverse unity?

The classic ecumenical vision, as I understand it (and in line with the first two chapters), is clearly the latter. To put it sharply, the point has not been to find ways of uniting Christian diversity but of recognizing, celebrating, and learning from the legitimate diversity of our given oneness. The past third of the century, however, has seen a shift toward far greater emphasis on diversity of both culture and confession. Much of this I applaud, for reasons that, hopefully, will become clear in this chapter. But there is also a danger in our era that the ecumenical goal of diverse *unity* will be obscured, and to the extent that happens, the movement's vision surely is impoverished.

51

* * *

First, a word of definition. The one church of Jesus Christ *must* include men and women of different races, ethnic identities, and cultural backgrounds. Diversity of this sort, Christians affirm, is God-given and, therefore, always to be embraced in the body of Christ. It goes without saying that this principle has been repeatedly violated—in Germany during the period of Nazism, in South Africa during the time of apartheid, in the United States during the years of segregation. But the ecumenical movement, though sometimes slow to act through its conciliar structures, has always known that genuine unity rests, as the New Delhi Assembly put it, on "the reconciling grace which breaks down every wall of race, color, caste, tribe, sex, class, and nation."[1] In this sense, the church is always inherently diverse. Denial of such diversity is, itself, an illegitimate diversity!

Thus, when ecumenists speak of the *problem* of unity and diversity, the diversity they have in mind is not so much that of race or sex but of such things as church structure, styles of worship, and theological formulation. How much diversity on *these* matters is consistent with the unity we seek?

There have, of course, been many moments in the history of the church when unity has been equated with uniformity of discipline, liturgical practice, and doctrinal affirmation; but this has never been characteristic of the modern ecumenical vision. Already in 1927, at the First World Conference on Faith and Order, Archbishop Söderblom spoke of the goal as "unity in multiplicity";[2] and since that time, "unity does not mean uniformity" has been an axiom of the movement.

The point I want to establish, however, is that diversity was seen as a mark of authentic unity, not as an end in itself. The focus was on manifesting the unity of *the church,* which is diverse, not on the diverse *churches,* which must be united. For example, the report of the Second World Conference on Faith and Order (Edinburgh, 1937) spoke of our given unity and then elaborated that "what we desire is the unity of a living organism, with the diversity characteristic of the members of a healthy body."[3] The Oxford Conference on Life and Work, also meeting

---

[1] In Michael Kinnamon and Brian E. Cope, eds., *The Ecumenical Movement: An Anthology of Key Texts and Voices* (Geneva: WCC; Grand Rapids, Mich.: Eerdmans, 1997), 89.

[2] H. N. Bate, *Faith and Order: Proceedings of the Lausanne World Conference* (Garden City, N.Y.: Doubleday, 1928), 331.

[3] Leonard Hodgson, ed., *The Second World Conference on Faith and Order* (New York: MacMillan, 1938), 252.

on the brink of World War II, spoke of diversity (especially of race, social status, and nationality), but added that the unity of this diverse fellowship "is not built up from its constituent parts, like a federation of different states." It is grounded in the sovereignty and redeeming acts of God, who is one and has made us one in Christ.[4]

A typical formulation of the period before 1960 is found in the writings of Suzanne de Dietrich, an early leader in the World Student Christian Federation and a founding staff member of the Ecumenical Institute at Bossey (discussed more fully in chapter 6). Dietrich, who has been called "the pioneer of ecumenical Bible study," focused frequently on Paul's image of the body. As Paul develops the metaphor in 1 Corinthians 12, difference is affirmed ("If the whole body were an eye, where would the hearing be?") but never allowed to become the basis of exclusion or separation, because the members are so completely interdependent ("The eye cannot say to the hand, 'I have no need of you'...If one member suffers, all suffer together with it."). Thus, wrote Dietrich, "the life of the body implies diversity in unity."[5] After all, the unity of those who are alike—those who have common interests, backgrounds, and perspectives—is hardly a distinctive witness! The world is filled with like-minded clubs and same-colored neighborhoods. The church shows that the Spirit is in it, the church serves as a sign of God's purposes, when it lives as a community of those who are not alike.

Although Paul is speaking of individual members of the church, the image is also applicable, Dietrich argued, to the interrelationship of communities. And when so applied, it reinforces what was said in chapter 2 about the crucial link between unity and renewal. It is through the sharing of diverse gifts that the one body of Christ is built up in truth and enabled to carry out its mission effectively. The question is not how the churches can move from present diversity into diversity-reducing unity, but how they can move beyond the limited unities of their present traditions into a unity that encompasses more of the diverse richness of the common Christian heritage.

This same position, affirming the diversity of our given unity, is found in the reports of early WCC assemblies. The delegates at Evanston (1954), for example, distinguished between diversity that is good "because it reflects both the diversities of gifts of the Spirit in the one body and

---

[4]J. H. Oldham, *The Oxford Conference: Official Report* (Chicago: Willett, Clark, 1937), 46.
[5]Suzanne de Dietrich, *The Witnessing Community* (Philadelphia: Westminster Press, 1958), 169.

diversities of creation by the one Creator" and diversity that changes into sinful division because it "disrupts the manifest unity of the body."[6] The New Delhi Assembly (1961) set forth its famous definition of unity as God's gift and then acknowledged that "unity does not imply simple uniformity of organization, rite, or expression...A lively variety marks corporate life in the one body of the one Spirit."[7]

It would be inaccurate not to acknowledge that the Roman Catholic Church has at times, through its official pronouncements, equated unity with uniformity. But it would also be inaccurate not to recognize the significant emphasis on diversity in Catholic discussions of unity since the beginning of the Second Vatican Council. Less than a year after the New Delhi Assembly, Pope John XXIII opened Vatican II by distinguishing between "the deposit of faith," on which Christians should be agreed, and "the way it is presented," on which they need not agree.[8] That was followed by the "Decree on Ecumenism" (1964), which echoed a venerable ecumenical axiom: "While preserving unity in essentials, let everyone in the church, according to the office entrusted to him, preserve a proper freedom in the various forms of spiritual life and discipline, in the variety of liturgical rites, and even in the theological elaborations of revealed truth. In all things let charity prevail."[9]

The difficulty, of course, comes in determining what is essential, but the scope of acceptable diversity seemed definitely to be expanding. In speaking of the disciplines of the Orthodox churches, the "Decree" suggests that, "far from being an obstacle to the church's unity, such diversity of customs and observances only adds to her comeliness"; and it goes on to apply this principle of "legitimate variety" to differences in theological expressions of doctrine.[10] The following words, spoken by John Paul II to a delegation of Coptic Christians, are typical of subsequent papal statements on the subject:

> It is fundamental for this dialogue to recognize that the richness of this unity in faith and spiritual life must be expressed in the diversity of forms. Unity—whether on the universal level or at

---

[6] In Lukas Vischer, ed., *A Documentary History of Faith and Order* (St. Louis: Bethany Press, 1963), 136.

[7] In Kinnamon and Cope, 89.

[8] See Harold E. Fey, ed., *A History of the Ecumenical Movement*, vol. 2 (Geneva: WCC, 1970), 330.

[9] In Kinnamon and Cope, 31.

[10] "Decree on Ecumenism," in *Doing the Truth in Charity*, ed. Thomas F. Stransky and John B. Sheerin (New York: Paulist Press, 1982), 29.

the local level—does not signify uniformity or the absorption of one group by the other. It is rather at the service of all groups, to help each one to give better expression to the gifts which it has received from the Spirit of God.[11]

Any call for uniformity, this implies, would simply be a call to universalize one form of Christian faith, and it would impoverish the church by denying the legitimate sharing of different gifts made possible through ecumenical contact. In 1970, the president of the Vatican Secretariat for Promoting Christian Unity, Cardinal Johannes Willebrands, urged Christians to conceive of unity as a "plurality of types" (in Greek, *typoi*) within the communion of the one, universal church.[12] The focus is still on unity, but a unity that is, by its very nature, marked by genuine variety.

* * *

At the same time that the Catholic Church was affirming diverse unity, several factors were contributing to a subtle but significant shift in emphasis within the WCC. For one thing, biblical scholars were now stressing the diversity of scripture. A WCC study in 1949 had stressed the Bible's theological unity and contended, without blushing, that a common reading of scripture could provide the basis for agreement on formerly contentious issues. Such optimism was severely shaken, however, at the Fourth World Conference on Faith and Order, held in Montreal in 1963, when addresses by Ernst Käsemann and Raymond Brown underlined the diversity of ecclesiologies in the New Testament. According to Käsemann, "the tensions between Jewish Christian and Gentile Christian churches, between Paul and the Corinthian enthusiasts, between John and early Catholicism are as great as those of our own day…To recognize this is even a great comfort and, so far as ecumenical work today is concerned, a theological gain."[13] Why? Because it frees us from a sterile preoccupation with recovering the shape of the New Testament church and opens us to the possibility of a unity that is richly diverse and oriented toward the future leading of the Spirit. To put it bluntly, the Bible, by its internal variety, actually canonizes the diversity of Christianity.

---

[11]In Stransky and Sheerin, 249.
[12]Johannes Willebrands, "Moving Towards a Typology of Churches," in Kinnamon and Cope, 99–101.
[13]In Kinnamon and Cope, 97.

Brown, while acknowledging significant theological differences within scripture, did not go nearly so far. "There are," he argued, "common elements found in all the ecclesiologies of the New Testament, and to neglect them in favor of diversity would be to fail to give a complete picture of the New Testament concept of the church."[14] It is probably fair to say that Brown's perspective carried the day in Montreal, but since then the pendulum has clearly swung toward Käsemann's position. By 1967, the Faith and Order Commission was ready to acknowledge that "awareness of the differences within the Bible will lead us towards a deeper understanding of our divisions and will help us to interpret them more readily as possible and legitimate interpretations of one and the same gospel." The variety of biblical witness reflects "the diversity of God's actions in different historical situations and the diversity of human response to God's actions"[15]—and is to be celebrated.

Subsequent studies by such biblical scholars as James D. G. Dunn (*Unity and Diversity in the New Testament*) and Oscar Cullmann (*Unity Through Diversity*) have underscored this point.[16] Cullmann, in a discussion of 1 Corinthians 12, goes so far as to suggest that "the richness of the full measure of the Holy Spirit consists in...plurality. Whoever does not reflect this richness, and wants uniformity instead, sins against the Holy Spirit."[17]

Alongside biblical scholarship, there was another, even more significant, factor contributing to the new emphasis on diversity: that is, the emergence of national cultures and churches that followed the collapse of colonialism. Eighteen so-called "younger" churches, eleven of them from Africa alone, joined the WCC in 1961. Add to this the fact that all of the Orthodox churches, Eastern and Oriental, were now part of the Council, along with the entry of the Catholic Church into the ecumenical movement with Vatican II (1962–1965), and the ecumenical picture was, indeed, becoming more diverse!

The Montreal conference on Faith and Order, with its debate between Brown and Käsemann, still spoke of *the* Tradition of the gospel, but it also affirmed the multiplicity of confessional traditions and

---

[14] In Kinnamon and Cope, 98.

[15] Quoted in Ellen Flesseman-Van Leer, *The Bible: Its Authority and Interpretation in the Ecumenical Movement* (Geneva: WCC, 1980), 40, 32.

[16] James D. G. Dunn, *Unity and Diversity in the New Testament: An Inquiry into the Character of Earliest Christianity* (Philadelphia: Westminster Press, 1977); and Oscar Cullmann, *Unity Through Diversity*, trans. M. Eugene Boring (Philadelphia: Fortress Press, 1988).

[17] Cullmann, 17.

cultures by which the one gospel is transmitted.[18] Since that time it has become commonplace to say that unity, far from being monolithic, must be "intercontextual," must involve the interrelatedness of contexts that are, *and will remain,* different. The impact of this conversation on the way ecumenists formulated the goal of visible unity was soon apparent. The WCC's Uppsala Assembly in 1968 lifted up the vision of a "dynamic catholicity" marked by "diverse ways of proclaiming the gospel and setting forth its mysteries…manifold ways of presenting doctrinal truths and of celebrating sacramental and liturgical events."[19] A subheading of the Uppsala report perhaps signals the shift more clearly than any other single phrase: "The *Quest* for Diversity."[20] Diversity, far from being a problem to be resolved, an appendix to the discussion of unity, is itself an imperative to be sought. Both unity and diversity are gifts of God. The church is both universal and particular. We betray its catholicity, the report implied, not by diversity but by conformity and parochialism.

The Nairobi Assembly in 1975 expanded on the work of New Delhi and Uppsala with its description of the unity we seek as a "conciliar fellowship of local churches which are themselves truly united" (i.e., able to share a common life of word and sacrament and to join in common prayer, witness, and service). This conception, said the delegates, "does not impose uniformity upon desirable diversity" but rather "cherishes and protects" the special gifts and insights accorded to local churches separated by space, culture, or time.[21] Uppsala's focus on catholicity helped describe the inner quality of life in the church, a quality that features diversity. Nairobi's focus on conciliarity began to explore the structure or discipline needed to maintain this diverse fellowship.

One sentence from the Nairobi report foreshadowed subsequent discussion: "It is because the unity of the church is grounded in the divine trinity that we can speak of diversity in the church as something to be not only admitted but actively desired."[22] Ecumenical theology had always been trinitarian, but new social interpretations of the doctrine, represented by such ecumenically engaged theologians as Jürgen Moltmann, emphasized the fellowship of distinct "persons" more than the unity of

---

[18]See "Scripture, Tradition and Traditions," in Kinnamon and Cope, 139–44.
[19]In Kinnamon and Cope, 95.
[20]Ibid., 94.
[21]Ibid., 110, 111.
[22]Ibid., 111.

the godhead. And it is not coincidental that discussion of the unity we seek began to focus on the Greek term *koinonia,* understood by many ecumenists as the fellowship or sharing of those who are, and will remain, different.

* * *

I hope that the history outlined above has been sufficient to show (1) that "since the Uppsala Assembly the issue of the relation of variety, or diversity, to the unity of the church has moved to the center of the debate,"[23] and (2) that a shift has occurred in the way the relationship is understood. The most prominent exponent of this new orientation, this new emphasis on diversity, is surely Konrad Raiser, who at the time of this writing is general secretary of the World Council. "Unity thinking," he argues repeatedly, has often been an instrument of domination. "Again and again in the course of church history, dissidents have been excluded or violently persecuted by invoking the 'unity of the church.'"[24] The idea of unity, which the Western church inherited from Roman culture, "almost inevitably leads to hierarchical systems of order" through which those with power claim their perspective as normative and insist on conformity.[25]

Behind Raiser's concern, if I understand him correctly, is the modern realization that differences of theology and practice are rooted in these God-given diversities of race, ethnicity, gender, and culture. To put it simply, people with different backgrounds and experience interpret the sources of the Christian faith diversely. Since unity has often meant a consensus, a suppression of such diversity based on the preferences of the powerful, the very term, Raiser contends, should probably be dropped from the ecumenical vocabulary. His emphasis is on the abiding difference of those who experience themselves in a solidarity we often call "communion," "fellowship," "*koinoinia.*" Such communion is not a static condition, but a dynamic process within which Christians grow in their sense of relatedness.

Raiser is certainly aware that unity as uniformity has been rejected from the beginning of the modern ecumenical movement. "And yet," he argued in an address to U.S. ecumenical leaders,

---

[23]Konrad Raiser, *Ecumenism in Transition: A Paradigm Shift in the Ecumenical Movement?* trans. Tony Coates (Geneva: WCC, 1991), 74.

[24]Ibid., 76.

[25]See Konrad Raiser, "Ecumenism in Search of a New Vision," in Kinnamon and Cope, 73.

there is a difference whether we speak of unity in diversity or of diversities related to one another in communion. In the first case the crucial question inevitably arises as to the limits of diversity; the maintenance of unity becomes the criterion for the recognition of the legitimacy of diversities. In the second case the crucial question becomes: how much "unity" is necessary and sufficient in order to maintain communion, and where does the pressure for unity become a threat to the expression of diversities within a living community?[26]

There is a great deal in Raiser's position that I find congenial with my own understanding of the ecumenical vision. I fully agree with his judgment that "many of the divisions in Christian history are not so much the result of deliberate separatism as of a rigid understanding of unity which perceived diversity as a threat."[27] Like him, I want to resist the notion that unity is synonymous with agreement. If by "communion" he means the visible, substantive interdependence—through shared worship, witness, and service—of those who claim Jesus Christ as their Lord and Savior and are baptized in his name, then I accept the word as an adequate (perhaps even preferable) substitute for "unity." Beyond that, his emphasis on diversity is an important corrective for a movement that, while saying "unity does not mean uniformity," has often still acted as if diversity were a problem to be resolved rather than a gift to be received and celebrated. The danger of what we might call "monolithic unity" is ever present, as friends who are struggling to remain in the Southern Baptist Convention frequently remind me.

But if monolithic unity is the Scylla of the ecumenical movement, "autonomous diversity" is its Charybdis. By autonomous diversity, I mean an approach to community that loses sight of its given wholeness in favor of the particularity of its parts. Diversity, understood as constitutive of unity, is a blessing. Diversity, seen as an end in itself, is simply another expression of the sinful human tendency to organize reality into homogenous enclaves.

If we *start* by emphasizing differences, then community is usually conceived of as peaceful coexistence, and it lasts as long as our interests are perceived to coincide. That, of course, is the pluralistic ideology of Western public life, and it often degenerates into a culture of narcissism in which groups, to borrow T. W. Adorno's famous phrase, retreat from

---

[26]Ibid., 74.
[27]Ibid., 73.

dialogue into "private reservoirs of the spirit" whenever it furthers their particular agenda. Pluralism in Christian perspective, however, is a relational concept implying mutual enrichment (the sharing of gifts). It assumes, that is to say, a fundamental unity from which we cannot, dare not, retreat.

It is not surprising that the new (over)emphasis on diversity has gone hand in hand with the notion that being ecumenical is synonymous with tolerance—a notion that I tried to repudiate in chapter 2. In addition to the problems discussed there, tolerance, if I read history correctly, is not able to stand the test of evil. All diversities are not legitimate; otherwise, we have no way of saying no to such groups as the Aryan Nation, which claims that its white supremacist ideology is Christian.

This is why "the limits of acceptable diversity" *is* the proper concern of ecumenism, including an ecumenical movement that values diversity.[28] Indeed, it is precisely our appreciation for, and commitment to, the God-given diversity of humankind (e.g., diversity of race, ethnicity, gender, and culture) that helps define limits of diversity with regard to theology and practice. God's yes to the world in all its particularity compels us to say no to ways of acting and thinking that threaten or deny our neighbors, each of whom bears God's image and for whom Christ died. This, I suspect, is what Orthodox theologian and ecumenical leader John Zizioulas (Metropolitan John of Pergamon) had in mind when he argued that "Eucharistic communion permits only one kind of exclusion— the exclusion of exclusions."[29]

Paul points in this direction when he urges the Roman congregations to "let love be genuine; hate what is evil, hold fast to what is good" (Romans 12:9). Genuine love knows when and how to hate, to oppose, those things that stand against its realization. To put it more sharply, there is in the Christian tradition a principled basis for refusing to tolerate intolerance, for refusing to include exclusivity. Given our sinfulness, this always risks betraying the message we wish to proclaim, but it is an unavoidable risk. Otherwise, our openness to diversity can mask what Herbert Marcuse called a "repressive tolerance" that allows racism and xenophobia to flourish in the name of diversity.

I have no doubt that Konrad Raiser, whom I deeply respect, would agree that unity and diversity must be held in dialectical tension in any

---

[28]See Michael Kinnamon, *Truth and Community: Diversity and Its Limits in the Ecumenical Movement* (Grand Rapids, Mich.: Eerdmans, 1988).

[29]*Orthodox Peace Fellowship Occasional Paper*, no. 19 (Summer 1994): 3.

theologically acceptable understanding of the church. An emphasis on unity that does not value diversity, including diversity of theological formulation, easily becomes bland and authoritarian; while an emphasis on diversity without a focus on the common good easily becomes fragmented and provincial. But in less able hands, Raiser's stress on diversity, typical of this era, runs the risk of impoverishing the ecumenical vision. The well-known Lutheran ecumenist Harding Meyer makes the same point in his recent book *That All May Be One: Perceptions and Models of Ecumenicity*. In most contemporary discussions on the subject, writes Meyer, "the idea of legitimate and necessary diversity seems...to have such a preponderance that the crucial question about the limits of diversity and with it the struggle for overcoming church-dividing differences—an absolutely central and necessary concern of the ecumenical movement—recedes into the background."[30]

* * *

One way to sum up, especially the arguments of chapters 2 and 4, is to emphasize that the vision of the ecumenical movement involves a necessary tension between truth and diverse community. Ecumenical thinkers have been accused, by Carl McIntyre and other outsiders, of promoting relativism. Those who insist that what is normal for them ought to be the norm for everyone else naturally think that ecumenical openness to diversity leads to doctrinal indifference, but this in no sense accords with the movement's self-understanding. "There is no gain in unity," said the delegates to the WCC's first assembly, "unless it is unity in truth and holiness."[31] "Nothing is so foreign to the spirit of ecumenism," according to the "Decree on Ecumenism," "as a false irenicism" that seeks compromise rather than truth in the face of theological contention.[32] The WCC's Toronto Statement addressed the matter directly.

There are critics, and not infrequently friends, of the ecumenical movement who criticize or praise it for its alleged inherent latitudinarianism. According to them the ecumenical movement stands for the fundamental equality of all Christian doctrines and concepts of the Church and is, therefore, not concerned with the question of truth.

---

[30]Harding Meyer, *That All May Be One: Perceptions and Models of Ecumenicity,* trans. William G. Rusch (Grand Rapids, Mich.: Eerdmans, 1999), 140.

[31]"The Universal Church in God's Design," in *Man's Disorder and God's Design,* The Amsterdam Assembly Series (New York: Harper and Brothers), 209.

[32]In Kinnamon and Cope, 33.

This misunderstanding is due to the fact that ecumenism has in the minds of these persons become identified with certain particular theories about unity, which have indeed played a role in ecumenical history, but which do not represent the common view of the movement as a whole, and have never been officially endorsed by the World Council.[33]

What the movement has endorsed is the idea that truth is best discerned through dialogue—understood as a mutually vulnerable pursuit of truth—in diverse community. I do not want to overstate the case. Not all diversities are complementary or mutually enriching. But there is an obvious bias toward this method.

A turning point (one scholar called it a "Copernican revolution") for ecumenical dialogue was the Lund conference on Faith and Order in 1952. Faith and Order's pre-Lund methodology is sometimes called "comparative ecclesiology"—the various traditions shared their doctrinal positions in order to discover whether each could recognize in others certain elements of the truth—and it often led, in the words of Lukas Vischer, to "carefully thought-out formulations which have different meanings for different people."[34] The Lund meeting, by contrast, spoke of a "Christological method." Instead of seeing the other ecclesial bodies as planets rotating around "our" center of truth, the churches were now encouraged to see Christ as the sun around whom all revolve.[35] The goal is not to compare truths (which invariably leads to defensive protection of our position), but to draw closer to Christ through dialogue with those who read scripture, tradition, and experience from angles other than ours.

Behind this is the assumption that no church comprehends and expresses, let alone lives, the full extent of the gospel. Yes, all churches claim to be faithful carriers of the apostolic tradition, and some emphasize that their bishops or other authoritative teachers have a special responsibility for promoting truth and discerning error. But, as I have tried to show in chapters 2 and 4, all churches involved in ecumenical dialogue acknowledge that they have things to learn from others.

The following arguments are found in numerous ecumenical texts: (1) God alone is sovereign. All human concepts, institutions, and activities stand under judgment of the One who finally transcends all our projects and explanations. (2) Human beings are finite and sinful.

---

[33]Kinnamon and Cope, 465.

[34]Vischer, *Documentary History*, 10.

[35]Ibid., 85–86.

Our perceptions, even of revealed truth, are always partial and in need of correction. (3) Christian faith is eschatological, which means that our historical existence must always be seen in light of God's ultimate purpose and promise.

> For my thoughts are not your thoughts, nor are your ways my way, says the LORD. For as the heavens are higher than the earth, so are my ways higher than your ways and my thoughts than your thoughts. (Isaiah 55:8–9)

> For now we see in a mirror, dimly, but then we will see face to face. Now I know only in part; then I will know fully, even as I have been fully known. (1 Corinthians 13:12)

"Both ecumenics and biblical studies," as Raymond Brown once put it, "should make us aware that there are other ways of being faithful to which we do not do justice."[36]

In trying to communicate this tension between truth and diverse community, this spirit of dialogue, I find myself returning to two giants of the movement: the Catholic Yves Congar and the Protestant Willem Visser't Hooft. "Ecumenism," according to Congar, "does not live by a purpose made up of doctrinal liberalism and of discarding, but of growth in a fuller and purer truth. And this it does by the hard road that encounters opposition from others, and leads to self-interrogation by each of us as we come face to face with our sources and with the truth."[37] Dialogue, wrote Visser't Hooft in several of his publications, is not negotiation but "a common struggle to arrive at a common mind about the truth that is in Christ…When we are concerned about the truth revealed in Christ, negotiation and compromise must be ruled out."[38] To put it another way, dialogue is a "spiritual battle for truth," but a common battle against error and not a fight between partners based on the assumption that one is already right and one wrong.[39] At their best, ecumenical Christians should be so committed to living the whole

---

[36]Raymond E. Brown, *The Churches the Apostles Left Behind* (New York: Paulist Press, 1984), 149.

[37]Yves Congar, "Ecumenical Experience and Conversion: A Personal Testimony," in *The Sufficiency of God,* ed. Robert C. Mackie and Charles C. West (Philadelphia: Westminster Press, 1963), 82.

[38]W. A. Visser't Hooft, *The Pressure of Our Common Calling* (Garden City, N.Y.: Doubleday, 1959), 74–75.

[39]W. A. Visser't Hooft, "Pluralism—Temptation or Opportunity?" *The Ecumenical Review* (April 1966): 147.

truth of the Christian faith that they readily confess that this truth is greater than any of their separated witnesses.

If the goal is tolerant cooperation rather than mutually critical growth in Christ, if theological diversity is affirmed as an end in itself rather than as a characteristic of truth-seeking community, then ecumenicity *does* do violence to the integrity of the faith and *does* contribute to the relativistic climate of our era. "There is all the difference in the world," writes theologian John MacQuarrie, "between a comprehensiveness that has seriously faced differences and sought to embrace the very truth expressed in the difference itself, and a vacuousness which, by accepting every point of view, denies any truth claim to all of them."[40] The first position is consistent with the ecumenical vision. The second most certainly is not.

---

[40]John MacQuarrie, *Christian Unity and Christian Diversity* (Philadelphia: Westminster Press, 1975), 47.

— 5 —

Unity and Repentance

Why "Growth" Is the Wrong Metaphor

The basic thesis of this chapter, like that of several previous chapters, is widely affirmed in principle but frequently violated in practice: Ecumenism requires (1) repentance for the ways we have borne false witness against our neighbors as well as false witness against the unity that is ours in Christ, and (2) conversion to a new way of seeing ourselves and others. This is, in a sense, a continuation of chapter 2 in which I suggested that ecumenism is a renewal movement. But whereas the concern in that chapter was to show how cooperation is not a fulfillment of the ecumenical vision, the concern here is to insist that ecumenism is not (or not simply) a matter of gradual "growth" in mutual recognition. It is a spiritual quest and, as such, is marked by a humble turning to God—and lots of surprises.

The ecumenical emphasis on renewal has already been well documented, and the explicit themes of repentance and conversion are equally prominent in literature from the movement. The First World Conference on Life and Work (Stockholm, 1925) summarized the point in an often-repeated sentence: "The closer we draw to the cross of Christ, the closer we come to each other."[1] Seen from the outside, the ecumenical

---

[1]Michael Kinnamon and Brian E. Cope, eds., *The Ecumenical Movement: An Anthology of Key Texts and Voices* (Geneva: WCC; Grand Rapids, Mich.: Eerdmans, 1997), 267.

movement may look like an endless series of meetings and texts, but ecumenical leaders have generally affirmed, to paraphrase Yves Congar, that the way to unity is on our knees. "The measure of our concern for unity," said the delegates to the WCC's Second Assembly (1954), "is the degree to which we pray for it. We cannot expect God to give us unity unless we prepare ourselves to receive his gift by costly and purifying prayer. To pray together is to be drawn together."[2]

It is hard to think of a major ecumenical figure who hasn't echoed this sentiment, but a particularly good example is the WCC's third general secretary, Philip Potter. "The ecumenical movement," said Potter in his address to the 1983 Vancouver Assembly, "is first of all a call to the churches to penitence, a change of heart and mind in the direction of the offer and demand of Christ."[3] The point is made more expansively in his book *Life in All Its Fullness*.

> There can be no unity without constant awareness of our limitations, our failures, our selfish attitudes and acts as individuals, societies, and churches. The prayer for forgiveness is the indisputable road to unity, because it places on us the inescapable responsibility to forgive one another, individually and corporately.[4]

Without this there can be no real sharing of gifts and, thus, no real renewal through mutual affirmation and admonition.

Potter's successor, Emilio Castro, was equally adamant on the importance of prayer and repentance, especially in his little book *When We Pray Together*. "Prayer," he wrote, "is the very heart of our being in the ecumenical movement."[5] Prayer gives us hope in the face of inevitable setback. Prayer reminds us of our connectedness to others who call on the name of Christ. Prayer opens us to the reality of God's grace and, thus, invites us "to offer our differences" in common service. Prayer involves a "humbling of ourselves" in order to recognize our shared identity as children of God.

Perhaps the best-known statement of this theme is found in the "Decree on Ecumenism," produced by the Second Vatican Council.

---

[2] *The Evanston Report: The Second Assembly of the World Council of Churches* (London: SCM Press, 1955), 91.
[3] In Kinnamon and Cope, 55.
[4] Philip Potter, *Life in All Its Fullness* (Geneva: WCC, 1981), 41.
[5] Emilio Castro, *When We Pray Together* (Geneva: WCC, 1989), 1.

"There can be no ecumenism worthy of the name," said the Catholic bishops,

> without interior conversion. For it is from newness of attitudes
> of mind, from self-denial and unstinted love, that desires for
> unity take their rise and develop in a mature way. We should
> therefore pray to the Holy Spirit for the grace to be genuinely
> self-denying, humble, gentle in the service of others, and to have
> an attitude of brotherly [and sisterly] generosity toward them.[6]

The bishops referred to this spiritual orientation as "the soul of the ecumenical movement," a point repeated by Pope John Paul II throughout his 1995 encyclical *Ut Unum Sint.* The commitment to ecumenism, he writes, "must be based upon the conversion of hearts and upon prayer, which will also lead to the necessary purification of past memories" (i.e., to a mutual forgiveness of past offenses). The Pope goes on to speak of a "dialogue of conversion," that involves "repentance and absolute trust in the reconciling power of the truth which is Christ."[7]

Earlier I made brief reference to Yves Congar, whose writings helped pave the way for the emphasis on Christian unity at Vatican II. Fr. Congar often wrote of the "ecumenical consciousness" as a consciousness of sin and, therefore, of repentance. It was, however, another Roman Catholic priest, Abbe Paul Couturier of Lyons, France, who probably did more than any other person to popularize this dimension of the ecumenical vision. Couturier is best known as champion of the Week of Prayer for Christian Unity, not unity through a return to Rome (as others had suggested) but unity "as Christ wishes and by the means which He desires." The ecumenical problem, as he saw it, has primarily to do with the orientation of our "inner life," with the need for prayer through which we see one another with the eyes of Christ.[8]

Couturier organized conferences of Catholics and Protestants at Presinge, which influenced the creation of Taizé (an ecumenical monastic community), and at the monastery of La Trappe des Dombes, which led to the formation of a widely respected dialogue and study committee, the Groupe des Dombes. Couturier's influence is still felt in the Groupe's 1991 document *For the Conversion of the Churches.* "Conversion is not simply at the source of the ecumenical movement, it represents its constantly

---

[6] In Kinnamon and Cope, 32.
[7] John Paul II, *On Commitment to Ecumenism,* para. 82.
[8] See Paul Couturier, "Prayer and Christian Unity," in Kinnamon and Cope, 498–503.

underlying motivation. When conversion flags, the ecumenical movement stagnates or goes into reverse."[9] The Second Vatican Council marked the official and institutional conversion of the Catholic Church to the ecumenical vision ("When the bishops saw that they were in agreement," writes Congar, "the Catholic Church converted to ecumenism in a few minutes or at most a few hours");[10] and, said the Groupe, such conversion is and must be the ultimate aim of the WCC.

The one church of Christ, which is God's gift sustained by the Holy Spirit, may be without spot or wrinkle. The historical churches, however, filled with sinful persons, have fought one another for worldly advantage, have acted like competing corporations instead of interdependent parts of a single body, have allowed secondary loyalties to override their shared commitment to Christ. How can the churches possibly speak of reconciliation or communion without confessing these sins to God and one another? There have been times when commitment to gospel truth has led Christians to break fellowship with others who claim Christ's name. Many divisions, however, have less noble roots: personal animosities, desire for power, fear of otherness. How can the churches possibly speak of unity without a public resolve to live, with God's help, in a different way?

* * *

This theme has by no means disappeared from ecumenical discourse, but there has been in recent years a curious split in the movement. The language of conversion and repentance is still used extensively in the Life and Work stream, but seldom in the recent literature of Faith and Order.

For example, the celebrated European Ecumenical Assembly (Basel, 1989)–convened as part of the global response to the WCC program Justice, Peace and the Integrity of Creation (JPIC)–included a major section on "Confession of Sin and Conversion to God" in its final report: "The precondition for any credible witness is conversion–conversion to the Creator who in his love cares for every single one of his creatures, conversion to Jesus Christ, the Son of God who in his life set us the example of true humanity, conversion to the Holy Spirit, the

---

[9]Groupe des Dombes, *For the Conversion of the Churches* (Geneva: WCC, 1993), 58.
[10]Quoted in Groupe des Dombes, 57–58.

source of new life."[11] And such language was echoed in the report of the JPIC world convocation, held a year later in Seoul, South Korea.

> To be sure, the focus in both meetings was on Christ's call to renounce mammon and to turn from behaviors that contribute to violence and oppression in the world. There are at least glimpses, however, of ecumenism's historic concern for Christian unity. The church, according to the participants in Seoul, is a "global community of mutual solidarity" which will increase only through a humble and radical reorientation on the part of the present church bodies.[12]

Renewal and conversion have also figured prominently in the last two WCC assemblies. The theme at Canberra (1991)–"Come Holy Spirit, Renew the Whole Creation"–took the form of a prayer. The theme at Harare (1998)–"Turn to God, Rejoice in Hope!"–named the need for conversion even more explicitly. Turning to God, said Brazilian theologianWanda Deifelt in her assembly address, means recognizing our solidarity with those who may be, to us, strange and threatening–such as the twenty-two million Africans now infected with the HIV virus. It means confessing our complicity in systems of economic inequity, the oppression of women, and environmental destruction. But once again, the theme of Christian unity is not entirely absent. "What message do we give to the world," she asked, "when Christians cannot speak with one voice against the injustices of our times?"[13] We have spent too much time and effort defining our differences while the world cries out for signs of God's kingdom. The churches, she claimed, must repent and be radically changed.

By contrast, in the Faith and Order stream of the movement, the way from visible division to visible communion is generally spoken of, at least in the past generation, as a process of gradual growth. The titles of recent, important publications are indicative: *Growth in Agreement, Progress in Unity? Growing Consensus.* One of the most widely studied ecumenical documents of recent years is "The Unity of the Church as

---

[11] *Peace With Justice: The Official Documentation of the European Ecumenical Assembly* (Geneva: Conference of European Churches, 1989), 45–48.

[12] "Final Document: Entering into Covenant Solidarity for Justice, Peace and the Integrity of Creation," in *Between the Flood and the Rainbow*, ed. D. Preman Niles (Geneva: WCC, 1992), 164–90.

[13] Wanda Deifelt, "Metanoia," in *Together on the Way: Official Report of the Eighth Assembly of the World Council of Churches*, ed. Diane Kessler (Geneva: WCC, 1999), 37.

Koinonia: Gift and Calling," written by the WCC's Faith and Order Commission and affirmed by the Canberra Assembly. Lukas Vischer, director of the Commission from 1965 until 1979, points out that this text makes only passing reference to repentance and no reference whatsoever to the need for conversion. Unity will increase through the patient accumulation of consensus until the day when, in the words of the text, "all the churches are able to recognize in one another the one, holy, catholic and apostolic church in its fullness."[14] "But," asks Vischer,

> does this quantitative view of fellowship correspond to reality? Will unity really be brought about by adding to it degree by degree until the vessel is full? Is it not much more likely that unity will be achieved, if at all, only if *all* the churches undergo a process of renewal? And, that being so, are not breaks inevitably to be expected along the way?[15]

The Canberra Statement, as it is commonly known, is certainly not an isolated instance. The Fifth World Conference on Faith and Order (Santiago de Compostela, 1993) displayed a kind of ecumenical schizophrenia. The worship at the meeting was dominated by a haunting refrain written by a Serbian Orthodox priest: "Tell us Lord. What has happened to us? Where did we go astray?" Nearly all of the speeches, however, concentrated on the gradual increase of communion through various forms of mutual recognition. The one notable exception, a brief presentation by longtime ecumenical participant Rena Karefa-Smart, makes my point through its own protest. We have gone astray, said Karefa-Smart, "by losing the vision of radical change that was shared by Brent and Mott and Brilioth and Bell and Ainslie [all great pioneers of the movement] and many others."[16] She contrasted the prevalent "towards visible unity" paradigm—in which "incremental gains, carefully chosen schedules, and imposing publications all add up to churches still separated in their ecumenical life"—with what she called "*koinonia* now." This latter orientation—which calls on the churches to live their given unity, not just work toward it—will require "a penitential spirituality that links confession and restitution with walking in new ways."[17]

---

[14]In Kinnamon and Cope, 124.

[15]Lukas Vischer, "Is This Really 'The Unity We Seek'?" *The Ecumenical Review* 44 (October 1992): 472.

[16]Rena Karefa-Smart, "The Future of the Ecumenical Movement: A Personal Reflection," in *On the Way to Fuller Koinonia: Official Report of the Fifth World Conference on Faith and Order*, ed. Thomas F. Best and Günther Gassmann (Geneva: WCC, 1994), 154.

[17]Ibid., 156, 159.

To my knowledge, the only bilateral theological dialogue on the international level to devote significant attention to "spiritual ecumenism" is that between the Christian Church (Disciples of Christ) and the Roman Catholic Church. The first volume of *Growth in Agreement,* a collection of reports from bilateral dialogues, lists "conversion" and "penitence" in its topical index; but, with the exception of the Disciples-Catholic report,[18] none of the references has to do with conversion or repentance on the part of the churches themselves.

I need to speak carefully. Those involved in ecumenical work have a great responsibility to teach about the faith of our neighbors, to lift up our ecumenical vision of church—and such work requires patience and sustained effort. But if communion "grows," it is surely because the Holy Spirit has convicted us of our sinful separations and converted us to see one another differently. Knowledge *about* the other, by itself, is not sufficient. In my experience, the language of growth often betrays an underlying conviction that unity is something we create or achieve (the Canberra Statement talks of how the churches "draw close to one another"), but this is neither sound theology nor an adequate depiction of ecumenical practice. Our "task" is to clear space—through dialogues, conciliar gatherings, common mission, and repentance—for the Spirit to act in our corporate life. Ecumenical Christians don't just prepare to grow; they prepare to be surprised! And they don't despair when progress is not steady or linear; they wait (however impatiently) on the Spirit, whose timetable may not fit their expectations.

Vischer is even more pointed: "The idea that a time could come when all the churches can also recognize in the others the fullness that they find in themselves is somewhat appalling; a fellowship of churches which lack nothing!"[19] This is what Albert Outler scorned as "ecumenism within the status quo," ecumenism without conversion or repentance—and it is not the vision that gave life to the movement.

* * *

In the last section of this chapter, I want to move the argument in a slightly different direction. One sign of conversion, as I see it, is a willingness to follow the leading of the Spirit, even when it means taking initiatives so bold that others regard them as foolhardy. There

---

[18]Harding Meyer and Lukas Vischer, eds., *Growth in Agreement: Reports and Agreed Statements of Ecumenical Conversations on a World Level* (New York: Paulist Press, 1984), 153–66.
[19]Vischer, "Is This Really 'The Unity We Seek'?" 473.

is a case to be made for prudent moderation, for a holy patience that builds a solid foundation of shared faith through painstaking dialogue– while waiting on the Spirit. I want also to contend, however, for a holy *im*patience that dares new things because we have been convicted of our sinful separation and infected with a vision of a transformed church.

There are numerous examples of such bold initiatives in the history of the movement. I want only to highlight two moments when the openness to conversion seems to have been particularly great. Historians may tell us that these initiatives were also driven by all-too-human considerations, but, to my eyes, they are Spirit led.

1. More than eighty years ago, in January of 1919, the Holy Synod of the Church of Constantinople, the Ecumenical Patriarchate, took an initiative that Willem Visser't Hooft called "without precedent in church history."[20] It decided officially to issue an invitation to all Christian churches to form a "league of churches" (*koinonia ton ekklesion*).[21] Let me repeat: This encyclical (primarily drafted by Archbishop Germanos, later to become one of the first presidents of the WCC) was sent "unto the *churches* of Christ everywhere"–the very appellation of "church" to another Christian body signaling the possibility of a new era.

The invitation, in addition to its call for a league or council of churches, contained other proposals that have since become standard ecumenical practice: a recommendation for dialogue, a denunciation of proselytism, a series of suggestions for very practical exchanges, an acknowledgment that some degree of rapprochement need not await the resolution of dogmatic differences, and the affirmation that we are already part of the one household of Christ and that our aim must be nothing less than full unity in him. This was not the stuff, in 1919, of prudent moderation and, perhaps for that reason, it did not generate much immediate favorable reaction. But by 1927, the Faith and Order conference in Lausanne was again raising the issue of a global league of churches, and by 1948 it had become a reality, at least for large parts of the Protestant and Orthodox families.

The encyclical was formally dispatched in January of 1920. In July of that year, the Anglican bishops meeting at Lambeth took a similarly bold initiative with their "Appeal to All Christian People." The conference

---

[20]W. A. Visser't Hooft, *The Genesis and Formation of the World Council of Churches* (Geneva: WCC, 1982), 1.

[21]In Kinnamon and Cope, 13.

acknowledged that all who believe in Jesus Christ and have been baptized in the name of the Holy Trinity share in the universal church. And in a stunning paragraph, the bishops also declared themselves ready to accept from the authorities of other churches a form of commission or recognition of their ministry.[22] This gesture placed Anglicans at the center of ecumenical discussion for the next generation.

These were not church responses to ecumenical texts. They were not prompted by a grudging acceptance of the need for cooperation. They were daring, humble, passionate appeals to common obedience— and they lifted the nascent movement to a new level of intensity.

2. Forty years later, in January of 1959, Pope John XXIII announced, to the surprise of the entire world (including, we are told, his closest advisors), the calling of an "ecumenical council." It was, he said, a sudden inspiration "like the spontaneous flower of an unexpected springtime."[23] The vision, personal sacrifice, and laborious work of such Catholic pioneers as Yves Congar, Max Metzger, Paul Couturier, Gustav Weigel, and George Tavard should not be minimized, but neither should the daring and novelty of this papal act. And the fact that the decision was made and announced before commissions got hold of it stirred the imagination of millions with promises of renewal. Equally bold was the Pope's address at the opening session of Vatican II, which, by distinguishing between the deposit of faith and its historical formulations, invited the Council to speak boldly and creatively to the age—with utterly miraculous consequences for relations among the churches.

A year after John XXIII's dramatic announcement, Eugene Carson Blake, convinced "that we cannot afford any longer the luxury of our historical divisions," invited the Protestant Episcopal Church, the newly formed United Church of Christ, the Methodist Church, and his own United Presbyterian Church "to break through the barriers of nearly 500 years of history" by forming a united church on American soil.[24] The Consultation on Church Union (COCU), created by Blake's prophetic sermon, despite occasional setbacks, has certainly fostered a greater level of ecumenical engagement in the United States.

---

[22]Kinnamon and Cope, 82–83.

[23]See Lukas Vischer, "The Ecumenical Movement and the Roman Catholic Church," in *The Ecumenical Advance: A History of the Ecumenical Movement,* ed. Harold E. Fey, vol. 2 (Geneva: WCC, 1970), 322.

[24]Eugene Carson Blake, "A Proposal toward the Reunion of Christ's Church," *The Christian Century* (December 21, 1960): 1508.

My point is that these initiatives are not examples of ecumenical "growth" but of radical obedience to the leading of the Spirit, however much it may disrupt our normal patterns of church life. The following sentences from COCU's theological consensus document are a fitting summary of this chapter:

> The particular traditions [that are coming together through the Consultation] have on occasion been distorted by false claims of exclusiveness and even of ultimacy. Thus, while church union involves preservation and sharing, it also requires repentance, conversion, and a new commitment by all to the enrichment coming from the gifts and experience of the other uniting churches.[25]

---

[25] *The COCU Consensus* (Consultation on Church Union, 1985), 11.

— 6 —

Ecumenism as Protest

Why Professionalization Undermines the Movement

One way of summarizing much of the argument from previous chapters is to point out that ecumenism, when true to its fundamental vision, is a protest movement. Ernst Lange, with his typical sharp-edged prose, calls it "the most massive domestic Christian protest against the way Christianity, by its alliance with the powers that be, [has] been transformed into its exact opposite."[1] Instead of common witness to the one Lord, competing denominations. Instead of renewal through the sharing of spiritual gifts, defensive protection of "our" gifts and agenda. Instead of common work for justice, separate (at times, contradictory) initiatives. Instead of a community that shows the world an alternative vision of human life, communities that parrot the surrounding culture's values and divisions.

It should not be surprising, therefore, that much of the impetus for, even leadership of, this protest movement, from its roots in the nineteenth century through the 1950s, came from laypersons, including such prominent figures as John R. Mott, J. H. Oldham, Robert Gardiner, Suzanne de Dietrich, Madeleine Barot, Hendrick Kraemer, Sarah

---

[1]Ernst Lange, *And Yet It Moves: Dream and Reality of the Ecumenical Movement,* trans. Edwin Robertson (Grand Rapids, Mich.: Eerdmans, 1979), 5.

Chakko, Kathleen Bliss, M. M. Thomas, Janet Lacey, and Nikos Nissiotis.[2] Laypersons are often less invested than ordained leaders in the status quo, more willing to experiment with new possibilities for church life and mission. Thus, as sociologist Bryan Wilson observed, dissenting movements within Protestantism have always been lay movements or "movements which gave greater place to lay[persons] than the traditional churches had ever conceded." Wilson also noted that, over the course of time, such movements are almost inevitably brought under the control of "full-time religious specialists"[3]–but that gets ahead of my argument.

There is probably no such thing as a "typical" ecumenical leader; but one layperson who exemplified the commitment to protest and renewal was Madeleine Barot. Barot was born in France in 1909 and, like many students of her era, became deeply involved during her youth in the Student Christian Movement (SCM)–in her case, at the Sorbonne, where she studied history. In conversations with her biographer, Andre Jacques, Barot claimed that the direction her life would take was shaped in large measure by the experience of meeting Christians from other countries and churches through the SCM, especially at the world conference of Christian youth, which met in Amsterdam on the very eve of the Second World War. "These were my friends no matter what happened–men and women united by the glorious affirmation of the conference theme: Christus Victor."[4]

The associate general secretary of the World Student Christian Federation at the time of the Amsterdam conference was Suzanne de Dietrich, another of the outstanding lay ecumenical leaders. In September of 1939, during the first weeks of the war, Dietrich challenged a joint meeting of French youth movements to come to the aid of persons displaced by the fighting–which led to the formation of the French refugee and relief organization CIMADE. Barot became CIMADE's first general secretary, at the age of thirty-one.

It was Barot who argued that such an organization should not be a matter of distant charity but of solidarity (a primary value for ecumenism); and so CIMADE teams, including Barot, lived in the

---

[2]See biographical entries in Nicholas Lossky et al., eds., *Dictionary of the Ecumenical Movement* (Geneva: WCC; Grand Rapids, Mich.: Eerdmans, 1991).

[3]Bryan R. Wilson, *Religion in Secular Society* (Baltimore: Penguin Books, 1969), 162.

[4]In Andre Jacques, *Madeleine Barot*, trans. Pat and Bill Nottingham (Geneva: WCC, 1991), 3.

refugee camps, attempting to provide both material and spiritual support. When deportations began, CIMADE worked closely with the Resistance to smuggle Jews across the borders into Spain and Switzerland. Through this, Barot developed a strong working relationship with Willem Visser't Hooft and the WCC "in process of formation" (as it was then called).

CIMADE was a Protestant organization, but by 1942 it was clear to Barot that there was an urgent need to coordinate the churches' resistance. "In the midst of political confusion," writes Jacques, "...a sense of brother and sisterhood brought Christians together to struggle, convinced that they were called to common witness."[5] This led to work with Roman Catholics, including the famous episode of "the Cardinal's children." On August 20, 1942, Barot and friends, with help from the Resistance, stole into a camp containing Jews scheduled for deportation and smuggled out eighty-four Jewish children whose parents signed papers giving legal custody to Cardinal Gerlier. The agreement included a promise that the children would be raised as Jews, and some of them were among the first French Jews to leave for Israel after the war.

Barot was invited to speak at the first major post-war ecumenical meeting—also a world student conference, this time in Oslo. She wrote the following in a preparatory article for that event:

> Young people aspire to Christian unity not only on the level of theological speculation and doctrinal affirmations but also on the level of daily life...It seems to them that beyond the reality of divided churches, the different ecumenical movements have created the consciousness of Christian unity, but that this remains too intellectual. To become a revolutionary and creative power at the heart of this broken world, the creative action of the Holy Spirit is needed.[6]

Many Christians, having served alongside sisters and brothers in Christ from other denominations and nations during the war, now found traditional church structures too restrictive. But war-time camaraderie is not enough. "We must," Barot wrote, "go beyond the stage of temporary manifestations of Christian life to find more permanent forms of relating to each other."[7]

---

[5] Jacques, 40.
[6] Ibid., 54–55.
[7] Ibid., 55.

Visser't Hooft had invited Barot to join the staff of the new World Council even before it was officially inaugurated, but she resisted leaving her more local and lay-oriented ecumenical work. "To prepare Christian laypersons to live out their faith," she wrote in 1950, "...is to give new life to the church...Work at CIMADE prepared team members for their vocation as laity, allowing them to find, even demand, their special place in a church always threatened by clericalism...CIMADE's originality, to be preserved at all costs, is to be a lay witness, a specific and ready service, an ecumenical place."[8]

In 1953, however, Barot finally agreed to become director of the newly created WCC Department on the Cooperation of Men and Women in Church and Society. Unity, she insisted, is not only a matter of Protestants and Catholics being reconciled, but of women and men experiencing the liberating equality and renewing complementarity that is theirs in Christ. The church, she wrote in an 1955 article for *The Ecumenical Review,* needs to ask itself "whether it is administering in the best possible way the spiritual gifts entrusted to it, whether it has not forgotten part of its message of liberation." The standards of the church must be different from those of the world because they are based on theological claims. If forcefully proclaimed, these gospel standards could "prove revolutionary as much for the secular world as for the church, leavening both throughout with new life."[9] The tone of protest is unmistakable.

* * *

The lay character of the early ecumenical movement can be overstated. The bold initiatives pointed to in chapter 5 were, in large measure, the work of ordained church leaders. Bishops, such as Nathan Söderblom and William Temple, gave crucial leadership during the first half of the century, and the great ecumenical conferences in Lausanne and Stockholm, Oxford and Amsterdam were largely dominated by professional theologians and ordained church officials. But, as historians often note, the movement's lifeblood flowed from the mission fields, the World Sunday School Association, the YMCA and YWCA, the various Bible societies, and the Student Christian Movement—all of which,

---

[8] Ibid., 59.

[9] Madeleine Barot, "Consideration on the Need for a Theology of the Place of Women in the Church," in *The Ecumenical Movement: An Anthology of Key Texts and Voices,* ed. Michael Kinnamon and Brian E. Cope (Geneva: WCC; Grand Rapids, Mich.: Eerdmans: 1997), 430.

as Keith Bridston observes, were marked by "their independence from ecclesiastical establishments, their character as voluntary associations, their simplicity of organization and operation, [and] their lay constituency."[10] In the nineteenth century, these movements were quite *un*denominational, which left the churches largely untouched. One way of demarcating the start of modern ecumenism is when these movements and groups became concerned not just with the extension of evangelism or with biblical literacy but with the reinvigoration of these things in the life of the church.

All this remained true during the time that the ecumenical movement was finding institutional form in such bodies as the WCC. Even before the official formation of the Council, the WCC's Ecumenical Institute at Chateau de Bossey was opened with the express purpose of renewing the church through revitalization of lay witness. In recent years, Bossey (as it is often called) has probably been best known for its semester-long graduate school program, which attracts pastors and seminary students from around the world. The focus in its early period, however, was on specialized meetings of laypersons from the same profession, including teachers, physicians, industrialists, artists, marriage counselors, journalists, and architects. "Since the Christian Church can face the troubled world of today only by the witness of a spiritually intelligent and active laity," wrote Bossey's first director, Hendrik Kraemer, "it is essential for the church resolutely to tackle this problem...It is only through her lay members that the church can live *in* the world without becoming *of* the world."[11]

Through its lay-oriented programs, Bossey was representative of a broader effort that included the German Kirchentag movement (initiated by a layman, Reinhold von Thadden-Trieglaff), lay institutes in such places as India and Zambia, and the network of European "lay academies"—all of which understood themselves as centers of renewal that cut across denominational boundaries. These institutes and academies arose after the war, wrote Kathleen Bliss, one of the notable lay leaders of the time, "because western culture and institutions are deeply secularized and alienated from Christian roots. The church in its institutional form is remote and irrelevant to society. The purpose

---

[10]Keith Bridston, "Domesticating the Revolution," in Keith R. Bridston and Walter D. Wagoner, *Unity in Mid-Career* (New York: Macmillan, 1963), 42.

[11]See Hendrik Kraemer, *A Theology of the Laity* (Philadelphia: Westminster Press, 1958).

of the institutes is to stimulate and instruct the laity to perform their own inalienable duty as people of God in the world of daily life."[12] Again, the note of protest rings clearly.

The idea that laity are the spearhead of the church's mission and primary agents of the church's renewal appeared in the reports of pre-WCC ecumenical conferences, especially the 1937 Oxford conference on Life and Work, which looked toward the day when the Spirit will cause "new life to break forth spontaneously" in small "cells" of lay Christians (an anticipation of today's "base communities").[13] Laypersons were not present in great numbers at the first three assemblies of the WCC, at least as official delegates, but the work of the laity figured prominently on the agenda of these meetings. For example, "The Laity–the Christian and His Vocation" was one of six overarching topics that shaped the assembly in Evanston (1954), and the link between laity and protest is certainly captured in the report from New Delhi (1961):

> [Since] this penetration of the world by the lay witness is an essential part of God's plan for [the] church, we must examine the conventional structures of our churches in order to see whether they assist or hinder the work of evangelism. We must not think of the "church" as primarily a building or as an enterprise run by ministers to which people come or are scolded for not coming. We must ask whether we do not too easily fall into the habit of thinking of the church as the Sunday congregation rather than as the laity scattered abroad in every department of daily life. We must inquire of ourselves whether our present structures do not preserve our divisions in a fossilized way, instead of enhancing the unity of the witnessing community.[14]

A committee on "The Significance of the Laity in the Church" was appointed at the first assembly in Amsterdam, but this was replaced following Evanston by a more permanent and prominent Department on the Laity. The department's publications–including its regular periodical, *Laity* (edited by Hans-Ruedi Weber and Madeleine Barot)– were for nearly two decades the most widely read materials published

---

[12]Quoted in Robert S. Bilheimer, *Breakthrough: The Emergence of the Ecumenical Tradition* (Grand Rapids, Mich.: Eerdmans, 1989), 125.

[13]J. H. Oldham, *The Oxford Conference: Official Report* (Chicago: Willett, Clark, 1937), 51.

[14]W. A. Visser't Hooft, ed., *The New Delhi Report: The Third Assembly of the World Council of Churches* (New York: Association Press, 1962), 88–89.

by the WCC. "In my view," writes Robert Bilheimer, who served on the World Council's staff from 1948 to 1963, "the most original aspect of ecumenical thought concerning the church's witness was its stress on the laity."[15] Writing in the *Dictionary of the Ecumenical Movement,* Elisabeth Adler concludes that "the rediscovery of the laity was probably the most important aspect of the renewal of the church in the 1950s and 1960s."[16]

And this was not only true for Protestants. The entry of the Roman Catholic Church into the ecumenical movement owed much to such ordained theologians as Fr. Yves Congar, Abbe Paul Couturier, and Fr. Gustave Weigel; but equally important was the witness (and pressure) of Catholic laypersons, including John Cogley, editor of the influential U.S. journal *The Commonweal.* In an article published in 1964 (the same year as the "Decree on Ecumenism"), Cogley maintained that just as war is too serious to be left to generals, so Christian unity is too important to be left to theologians! Theological dialogue has an indispensable part to play. "But only the laity can create the climate of mutual trust and charity for the dialogue to be effective."[17]

Beyond that,

> ...it might even be said that it is the work of contemporary
> laymen [and laywomen] to undo some of the mischief caused
> by theologians in the past. For when we ask ourselves how the
> scandalous division of Christendom came about, the burden
> of responsibility seems to fall more heavily on the clerics and
> religious professionals than on the ordinary [person]-in-the-pew.[18]

One expression of lay ecumenical involvement in North America—including Catholics, Protestants, and Orthodox—was the program of "living room dialogues," sponsored by the Division of Christian Unity of the National Council of Churches and the (Roman Catholic) Apostolate of Good Will of the Confraternity of Christian Doctrine. During the mid-1960s, more than five thousand dialogue groups gathered once a month in living rooms throughout the U.S. and Canada for Bible study, prayer, and conversation about the state of the church. "The purpose," according to published dialogue materials, "is to help individual laymen and

---

[15]Bilheimer, 125.

[16]Lossky, 580.

[17]John Cogley, "Ten Commandments for the Ecumenical Age," in *Steps to Christian Unity,* ed. John A. O'Brien (Garden City, N.Y.: Doubleday, 1964), 244.

[18]Ibid., 244–45.

women become personally concerned about Christian unity and to pray for the reunion of all Christians...Normally, it is expected that no priest or minister will be present at these sessions"[19]–though they might later be consulted to answer questions stemming from the dialogue.

* * *

Things were changing rapidly, however, as the turbulent 1960s drew to a close. The laity department was phased out in the 1971 restructuring of the WCC, and the subject of lay vocation as a crucial dimension of ecumenical renewal has rarely been broached in major meetings of the Council over the past thirty years. "'The laity' has almost disappeared from ecumenical discussion," wrote Konrad Raiser in a 1993 issue of *The Ecumenical Review.* "This is all the more striking because 'laity' was an ecumenical keyword only a generation ago. Since then the passionate enthusiasm of the early ecumenical movement–which in several important respects saw itself as a lay movement–has somewhat abated."[20]

As Raiser pointed out, this shift is very visible in ecumenical discussions of ministry. In the two decades following the formation of the WCC, Faith and Order documents on the subject included extensive treatment of the ministry of the laity. By contrast, the ministry section of *Baptism, Eucharist and Ministry,* sent by Faith and Order to the churches in 1982, contains only six paragraphs (out of fifty-five) that deal with "the calling of the whole people of God." Lay ministry hardly appears in the index of *Growth in Agreement,* a comprehensive collection of bilateral dialogue reports from 1971–82, because the focus of these reports is not on renewal but on resolution of specific areas of doctrinal disagreement. Indeed, the methodology of these dialogues–conversations among theological experts that must then be "received" by the laity– reinforces the notion that laypersons are passive spectators in the effort to realize visible church unity.

There are several reasons for this development. For example, the entry of the Roman Catholic Church into the arena of ecumenical dialogue had a profound, though somewhat mixed, impact. The Second Vatican Council emphasized both "the apostolate of the laity" and spiritual renewal as the foundation of ecumenism, but dialogues involving

---

[19]William B. Greenspun and William A. Norgren, eds., *Living Room Dialogues* (Paramus, N.J.: Paulist Press, 1965), 8.

[20]Konrad Raiser, "Laity in the Ecumenical Movement," *The Ecumenical Review* 45 (October 1993): 375.

the Catholic Church have tended to focus on the proper ordering of, and apostolic succession in, ordained ministry.

The same can be said for the full involvement of Orthodox churches in ecumenism following the WCC's New Delhi Assembly. According to Orthodox theology, all members of the church are qualitatively equal, and all are needed for the *pleroma* (wholeness, fullness) of the body of Christ. In fact, argued Nikos Nissiotis (himself an example of the Orthodox tradition of lay theologians), the distinction between clergy and laity is a "recent invention" that goes hand in hand with churchly division.[21] Having said this, however, it is also true that Orthodox delegations to ecumenical conferences are generally dominated by members of the clerical hierarchy.

Somewhat ironically, the increased concern for human liberation has also contributed to the lessened emphasis on laity, at least in my reading of ecumenical history. For one thing, the idea of gradually influencing social structures through the daily witness of laypersons—a key motif of Oxford, Evanston, and early Bossey conferences—gave way, in global ecumenical settings, to the call for radical, immediate social change. For another, the historic concern for laity was increasingly split into movements that sought the empowerment of specific groups, such as women, youth, the poor, and persons with disabilities. The keyword was now "participation," with "laity" listed alongside other components of participatory community. Philip Potter's address as WCC general secretary to the Vancouver Assembly in 1983, perhaps the classic ecumenical statement on participatory community, devotes only a single sentence to explicit concern for lay leadership in the church.[22]

There is obviously much to celebrate about the higher profile of women and youth in ecumenical thinking. The women's movement, to take that example, is certainly a protest against the state of the church. The problem, however, is that even when such efforts are concerned with the renewal of the church as a whole, they can be pigeon-holed under the heading "special interest." A movement for renewal that is driven by laity—women and men, young and old—is harder to marginalize or ignore.

---

[21] Nikos Nissiotis, "The Charismatic Church and the Theology of the Laity," in Kinnamon and Cope, 440.

[22] Kinnamon and Cope, 57.

An even more problematic development, however, is the professionalization (which usually means the clericalization) of the ecumenical movement itself. Many churches now have specialized offices for handling "ecumenical affairs" that have become highly institutional—for example, handling relationships with councils of churches and overseeing official participation in sanctioned theological dialogues. All of this is inevitable and, in many respects, positive. Movements, if they are to be sustained across generations, must assume some institutional form. But the form the ecumenical movement has taken has had the effect of marginalizing laity and muting the protest character of the movement's animating vision.

To put it bluntly, ecumenism has been, to a large extent, domesticated, brought under control, by the churches it was intended to reform. "For my generation," lamented Visser't Hooft in 1974, "the ecumenical movement had all the attraction of something unexpected and extraordinary. For the present generation, it is simply part of the church's design."[23] Lange is less restrained. "My own personal ecumenical experience," he writes in *And Yet It Moves,* "was acquired…within the laity and renewal movements, which originally invented the ecumenical movement in the nineteenth century but were then swallowed up and alienated by it as the church institutions took over."[24] As he sees it, "technocrats," with a focus on short-term objectives, have replaced visionaries, to the movement's great impoverishment.

I quote this last passage because I am convinced that Lange is basically on target, but the point needs to be made in a more nuanced way. I am very thankful for the work done by ecumenical offices and officers. Their faithfulness, in my experience, is beyond question; they should not be dismissed as "technocrats." I am also thankful that churches, not just committed individuals, are now key participants in the work of ecumenism. But the basic point remains: Ecumenism cannot be left for denominational specialists and theological experts to do on our behalf. It cannot be something that the laity leave for the clergy to worry about. Unless the movement becomes less clericalized, less dominated by "professional ecumenists," ecumenism will seem increasingly remote and irrelevant to persons in our congregations—and its protest character will be further diminished.

---

[23]W. A. Visser't Hooft, *Has the Ecumenical Movement a Future?* (Belfast, Ireland: Christian Journals Ltd., 1974), 40–41.

[24]Lange, 66.

* * *

This last discussion points, of course, to the classic tension between "movement" and "institution." Movements are generally marked by flexible forms of organization, a high degree of personal commitment, and a strong sense of vision (which outsiders may regard as utopian). All of this is inevitably tempered, however, by a desire for continuity and the reliability of ongoing structure. The following quotation from a biography of the WCC's first general secretary captures my own position:

> From his early days onwards, W. A. Visser't Hooft realized that it was important, for the health of the ecumenical movement, that the institutional, clerical form of ecumenism and the "unfettered," imaginative ecumenism of laity, youth and women recognize each other's *raison d'etre*. Both are needed. Ecumenical history shows that groups of individuals fired by the vision of a renewed and united people of God can render great service. But the vision will only become a substantial reality when it takes shape through the life of historical church bodies.[25]

The point I have tried to make in this chapter is that the creative tension between these groups is not holding. There are plenty of lay-driven, Christian movements concerned with such things as protecting the environment, obtaining debt relief for poor countries, and promoting the rights of oppressed minorities in church and society. But these often do not identify themselves in any way with concern for a renewed and united church. Meanwhile, church unity is increasingly left to those whose profession it is to worry about it.

Much has been accomplished over the past generation through official church-to-church dialogues, and much has been gained over the past two generations through the official participation of churches in conciliar ecumenism (a point I will focus on in the next chapter). The task for the next generation will be to celebrate and deepen such church involvement *while also* making more room for volunteer, lay-led movements, and emphasizing education for ecumenism among the laity.

Konrad Raiser, who has often lamented the "institutional captivity" of the ecumenical impulse, has suggested that the WCC help develop

---

[25]Ans J. van der Bent, *W. A. Visser't Hooft: Fisherman of the Ecumenical Movement* (Geneva: WCC, 2000), 34.

a wider "forum" of Christian churches and ecumenical organizations.[26] Such a forum might preserve the Council's integrity as a fellowship *of churches* while also providing space for other voices to be heard. While the jury is still out on that particular idea, one thing seems clear: If the *protest* character of this *movement* is silenced, ecumenism will not just be impoverished—it will have lost its essence.

---

[26]See Konrad Raiser, *To Be the Church: Challenges and Hopes for a New Millennium* (Geneva: WCC, 1997), chap. 6.

— 7 —

Councils of Churches

Why They Are Not Structures Alongside the Churches

A chapter on councils of churches may seem out of place in a book that has been dealing more abstractly with the vision of the ecumenical movement. Councils of churches, however, are the single most visible expression of modern ecumenism. It is my conviction, therefore, that a discussion of the nature and purpose of councils can tell us much about the movement as a whole. Beyond that, I am convinced that councils of churches are widely misunderstood, and that this contributes to the enervation that some of them are now experiencing.

It is important to keep in mind throughout this chapter that councils of churches are a new thing in the history of Christianity. Prior to the beginning of the ecumenical movement in the early twentieth century, there were organizations of Christians dedicated to particular tasks (e.g., Bible societies and the YMCA). Many contemporary councils have their roots in these organizations. But when churches commit themselves *to one another* for common service, witness, study, and (occasionally) worship, something new is coming into existence—something that is beyond the divisions of the past but not yet the "visible unity in one faith and one eucharistic fellowship" we seek. Conciliarity, wrote Orthodox theologian Nikos Nissiotis, "is a quite new phenomenon and we have at our disposal no appropriate ecclesiological terms to describe it. We here have to face a reality that goes beyond our capacity to conceptualize it theologically."[1] Or as Willem Visser't Hooft succinctly put it, "We try to define ecumenical realities in the thought-forms of the pre-ecumenical age."[2]

There have been a number of attempts to fill this theological void over the past half century. The most influential document on the theology of councils of churches is the so-called Toronto Statement, drafted by the WCC's Central Committee in 1950 (two years after the inauguration of the Council itself). The discussion was taken up again by the Fourth World Conference on Faith and Order (Montreal, 1963) in response to the new involvement of Orthodox churches in conciliar ecumenism and the anticipated involvement of the Roman Catholic Church as a result of Vatican II.

Since that time, the WCC has sponsored three international consultations for national and regional councils and, in recent years, has reflected extensively on its own meaning and purpose through a study process called *Towards a Common Understanding and Vision of the World Council of Churches* (CUV). Other councils have undertaken a similar study. National councils in such places as Great Britain and Australia underwent major transformations during the 1990s following theological reflection, and, in the United States, the National Council of the Churches of Christ (NCCC) authorized an Ecclesiology Study Task Force to report on "the ecclesiological meaning of membership in the NCCC."

In my opinion, the single most significant point to emerge from all of this discussion is the following: The essence of a council of churches is the relationship of the member churches to one another, not their relationship to the structure of the council. To put it another way, the essence of a council is not so much what the churches *do* together as what they *are* together.[3]

The seminal statement is a deceptively simple phrase from the "Basis" of the WCC: "The World Council of Churches is a *fellowship* of churches."[4] There are a lot of significant organizations that provide services on behalf of the churches. These should not be confused,

---

[1]Nikos Nissiotis, "Christian Councils and Unity of the Local Church," *One in Christ*, no. 2 (1972): 163.

[2]Michael Kinnamon and Brian E. Cope, eds., *The Ecumenical Movement: An Anthology of Key Texts and Voices* (Geneva: WCC; Grand Rapids, Mich.: Eerdmans, 1997), 495.

[3]See Diane Kessler and Michael Kinnamon, *Councils of Churches and the Ecumenical Vision* (Geneva: WCC, 2000), chap. 3.

[4]In Kinnamon and Cope, 469.

however, with a council, a fellowship, of the churches themselves. Whenever churches see a council as "them" rather than "us" (as "that organization" rather than "our fellowship"), then conciliar life has been radically misunderstood. Without a recognition of this insight, churches tend to avoid the accountability that ought to go with membership in a council of churches. The NCCC's Ecclesiology Study report underscores this idea forcefully.

> Repeatedly it is said that the NCCC needs to be transformed. Of course, every ecumenical body needs periodically to be renewed...However, if the ecumenical witness of the NCCC is not what it ought to be, then it is not just "the council" that needs to be transformed but also the churches. The Council can be restructured without ever touching the fundamental ecclesiological question of our churches' relationship to one another.[5]

A council's structure may need reform, even drastic change. The *basic* question, however, is whether the ecumenical commitment of the member churches, their willingness to live in deeper fellowship with one another, is adequate to the imperatives of the gospel.

Not all councils, I must acknowledge, identify themselves as a "fellowship" of churches. A recent study of local and regional ecumenism in the United States confirms that these organizations are, generally speaking, the venue through which congregations or denominations cooperate to meet human needs. Their concern is less to be a fellowship of churches on the way toward fuller communion than "to do together what cannot be done at all or as effectively alone."[6] It is my experience, however, that some local councils are now seeking a deeper ecclesial identity and that most local ecumenical leaders agree that a council is "more than a mere functional association of churches set up to organize activities in areas of common interest."[7]

I also recognize that not all churches mean the same thing when they become part of a council that is defined as a fellowship or community of churches. The (Orthodox) Ecumenical Patriarchate, in its contribution to the CUV process, called for a clarification of the term

---

[5]Unpublished report. Quoted in Kessler and Kinnamon, 20.
[6]Gary E. Peluso, "The Crisis of Local and Regional Ecumenism," *Mid-Stream* 32 (October 1993): 8–12.
[7]*Towards a Common Understanding and Vision of the World Council of Churches* (Geneva: WCC, 1993), para. 3.2.

fellowship when used in relation to conciliar membership;[8] and an inter-Orthodox consultation on CUV explicitly denied that the WCC, despite the language of fellowship, has an "ecclesial character." "It is presently a valuable instrument for the member churches which serves the churches in their movement toward unity."[9] But this cautious assessment seems somewhat belied by the actions of the Orthodox. If the WCC is not more than a secular organization, comparable to intergovernmental bodies such as the United Nations, why insist, as Orthodox churches frequently do, that the Council's social decisions be grounded in shared faith? Why insist, as Orthodox churches did prior to joining the WCC in 1961, that the Basis include a confession of faith in the trinity? In 1992, the Eastern Orthodox churches temporarily suspended their participation in the U.S. national council, citing problematic decisions taken *within* other member churches. If the NCCC is not more than a utilitarian structure, why pay such attention to the internal life of others involved in it?

All of this rests, finally, on the argument made in chapter 1. A fellowship is not something *we* can create. The term reminds us that, thanks to what God has done, our churches are not strangers to one another, whatever their historical separations. Councils are, in this sense, the place where, because of their given unity in Christ, churches seek to grow in fellowship through the experience of "living contact with each other" (Toronto). "We cannot seek for what we do not know at all," wrote Albert Outler. "And if we already know, even in part, the reality and joy of unity-in-Christ, then it is from that concrete, personal experience that we must learn about the fullness of unity which we do not yet know."[10] "We are above all," said Visser't Hooft to the delegates at the Amsterdam Assembly, "a fellowship which seeks to express that unity in Christ already given to us and to prepare the way for a much fuller and much deeper expression of that unity."[11] This, as I read the documents, is the essential premise behind councils, especially at the world and national levels.

* * *

[8]Thomas FitzGerald and Peter Bouteneff, eds., *Turn to God—Rejoice in Hope: Orthodox Reflections on the Way to Harare* (Geneva: WCC, 1998), 63.
[9]Ibid., 56.
[10]Albert C. Outler, *The Christian Tradition and the Unity We Seek* (London: Oxford University Press, 1958), 154.
[11]W. A. Visser't Hooft, *Memoirs* (London: SCM Press, 1973), 210.

This basic point—that "the essence of the Council is the relationship of the churches to one another," that the council *has* a structure but *is* a fellowship—has been underscored in both the CUV text and the NCCC Ecclesiology Study report, but it has apparently never really been internalized by the churches or their leaders. The problem was named with great clarity by Victor Hayward, who, in the late 1960s and early 1970s, was responsible for relationships between the WCC and national councils of churches. After visiting nearly every national council on the planet, Hayward wrote the following in a memorandum to then-general secretary, Eugene Carson Blake:

> The key issue is that most churches show only partial commitment to what is involved in being a fellowship of churches. Where there is commitment, it is often to the council as an institution and not to the other churches that comprise its membership. Most councils, thus, are an ecumenical facade behind which churches remain as unecumenical as ever.[12]

David Gill, general secretary of the Australian Council of Churches, similarly decries "the notion that churches, having demonstrated that their hearts are in the right place by joining an ecumenical body, can now leave ecumenism to the council and get on with denominational business-as-usual. Councils of churches set up to be ecumenical instruments can all too easily degenerate into ecumenical alibis."[13] Churches are often all-too-ready to leave ecumenism to "the council"—as if conciliar membership means that they have hired persons to be ecumenical for them! When this happens, councils lose their ecumenical significance.

The WCC has had a stronger focus on Christian unity than most national or local councils, but even here the idea of being a fellowship of churches often takes a back seat to the idea of being a program agency. "All activities of the Council," writes Konrad Raiser, "should be in relation to the purpose of strengthening relationships between churches. Over the past decades, by contrast, relationships and communication have been understood as a support function of the programmatic work

---

[12]Unpublished memorandum.
[13]David M. Gill, "Whom God Hath Joined Together: Churches and Councils of Churches," *The Ecumenical Review* 42 (January 1991): 47.

of the WCC."[14] Even the CUV text, in several places, uses the old language of us and them: for example, "This document...is intended to help churches to evaluate their own ecumenical commitments and practice, both in their own immediate context and in *their relationships to the WCC*"[15] (rather than "to one another through the WCC").

The national council in the United States came into existence, two years after the WCC, as a merger of largely autonomous program units with distinct purposes and constituencies. It is hardly surprising, therefore, that its original *Constitution* read that the NCCC is a "cooperative agency for the churches." This was finally changed in 1981 to say that the NCCC is "a community of Christian communions" that "covenant with one another to manifest ever more fully the unity of the church." But even then the revised *Constitution* said that "*the Council* brings these communions together in common mission"[16]—as if the NCCC were primarily an office in New York instead of the churches in community with one another.

Why do the churches prefer to keep councils as program agencies and to deny them ecclesiological significance? Part of the reason surely has to do with what former NCCC general secretary Arie Brouwer called the "ideology of denominational churchliness." Just as the ecumenical movement began as a renewal effort, so the denominations are best understood, argued Brouwer, as "reform movements within the one church of Christ which are temporarily 'denominated' or named according to the reforms they embody,"[17] until such time as those reforms are received into the bloodstream of the church as a whole. The problem is that, instead of ceasing to exist as separate bodies once their reforming purpose has run its course, denominations begin to see themselves as ends in themselves—and they do so by asserting their own churchly character, with obvious consequences for ecumenical fellowships.

Brouwer put it this way: "Claiming churchliness for themselves alone, the denominations continue to deny to councils and other instruments of unity the ecclesial significance that would empower them to challenge

---

[14]Konrad Raiser, *To Be the Church: Challenges and Hopes for a New Millennium* (Geneva: WCC, 1997), 101.

[15]*Towards a Common Understanding,* Introduction.

[16]National Council of the Churches of Christ U.S.A., *Constitution,* preamble.

[17]Arie R. Brouwer, "The Real Crises at the NCC," *The Christian Century* (June 27–July 4, 1990): 632.

the continuing separate existence of the denominations."[18] The point has scriptural support. "Church," in the New Testament, means either the locally gathered community or the universal body of Christ. Denominations are intermediate mission structures that can help transmit the faith and expand the circle of Christian service, unless they claim, implicitly or explicitly, they be the only legitimate expressions of church and, thus, prevent Christians from living more fully together in each place. The former director of the state council of churches in New York, Arleon Kelley, is even more pointed:

> The modern conciliar model was an early twentieth-century dream to bring unity among the churches, but as it was developed and institutionalized in the United States, it could not be a better designed instrument to protect denominational prerogatives. Why? Because councils have been organized in such a way as to protect each member church's claims that they are church, while obscuring the conciliar goal of mutuality, where the churches, together, are "the church."[19]

This needs to be said carefully. A council of churches is not the church. Councils do not bind members in eucharistic communion; they are not responsible for Christian initiation; they do not ordain a ministry of word and sacrament. Actions taken in a council of churches are authoritative, as William Temple wrote in preparation for the founding of the WCC, only to the extent that these actions bear the intrinsic authority of wisdom and truth.[20] Councils of churches, however, are at least "preliminary expressions" (Vancouver Assembly) of deeper and wider fellowship. A small conference, organized by the Vatican and the WCC in 1982, suggested that a council "provides an ecclesial situation in which inherited values and elements of separated churches are tested and discerned and in which there is a real though imperfect experience of the future diversity of full conciliar fellowship."[21] Brouwer goes further: "Just as the church is given by the Spirit as sign, instrument, and foretaste of the kingdom, so are the councils given by the Spirit as

[18]Arie R. Brouwer, *Overcoming the Threat of Death* (Geneva, WCC, 1993), 102.
[19]Unpublished essay.
[20]See W. A. Visser't Hooft, *Has the Ecumenical Movement a Future?* (Belfast, Ireland: Christian Journals Ltd., 1974), 45.
[21]"The Significance and Contribution of Council of Churches in the Ecumenical Movement," *Mid-Stream* 22 (April 1983): 224.

signs, instruments, and foretastes of the church."[22] A council is not the church, but it can remind the denominations that they are not the church either—at least not the one, holy, catholic, and apostolic body of Christ that is our gift and calling.

Such an argument is often resisted, however, not only by the Catholic and Orthodox churches (which do claim, in some sense, to be *the* church) but also by Protestants who treat ecumenism as something tacked on to their "real" work and identity. In my experience, conciliar membership rarely alters a church's self-understanding. We are willing to participate, to the extent resources allow, but seldom recognize councils as *us,* as manifestations—or at least anticipations—of the church.

Thus far, I have been talking about how churches, through their leaders and representatives, often think of councils as bodies apart from themselves. It is also true, however, that the staff or assembly of a council structure may act and speak as if the council were something alongside of, even over against, the churches. When I worked at the WCC, my colleagues and I were often guilty of thinking that *we* were the Council and that we knew what was good for the churches, even if they didn't want what we had to offer.

This also needs to be said carefully. The pioneers of modern ecumenism understood councils to be *both* instruments of the churches *and* instruments of the ecumenical movement. Lange put it this way with regard to the World Council:

> On the one hand, it is an instrument for international cooperation between the churches; in this role it has to implement the concrete decisions of its members, nothing more. On the other hand, it is the *avant-garde* of reunited Christendom, and an anticipation of coming union and renewal, a post-dated check; in this role it has to think, speak and act prophetically, to challenge the churches and to set them moving.[23]

This means that the staff perform tasks that the churches specifically authorize, but they also are called to push beyond what the churches may initially identify as their common agenda. If churches cling to marks of division, then isn't it the duty of council leaders, precisely as the

---

[22]Arie Brouwer, "The Church, the Churches, and Councils of Churches," *Reformed Review* 44 (Winter 1990): 131.

[23]Ernst Lange, *And Yet It Moves: Dream and Reality of the Ecumenical Movement,* trans. Edwin Robertson (Grand Rapids, Mich.: Eerdmans, 1979), 136.

churches' faithful servants, to challenge the churches to deeper and more costly ecumenical commitment? Councils, writes Lukas Vischer, are "the thorn in the flesh of the churches. They are a constant reminder to the churches of the anomalous situation in which we live. They prod the churches to expose themselves continually to the power of the Holy Spirit. They constitute the setting, created by the churches themselves, within which the promise of renewal may be heard."[24]

The point I am making, however, is that the work of "the council" will likely be dismissed or resisted unless the churches recognize that the challenge, the thorn, comes from their mutual commitment to one another—not from some group of professional ecumenists. To put it another way, the fellowship experienced in conciliar ecumenism is not only rooted in what the churches are but in what they are called to become. Through their membership, churches should expect—should demand!—to be challenged to deeper commitment *by one another.* A central purpose of the staff and structure of a council is to hold the churches accountable to the commitments they make by virtue of their participation in this fellowship.

There is a related point that deserves emphasis. The fellowship that is at the heart of a council of churches "is not something abstract and static" but "a dynamic, relational reality,"[25] which ought to change and, hopefully deepen as a result of common membership in the council. The Toronto Statement said that no church is obliged to change its ecclesiology as a *consequence* of membership in the World Council.[26] This affirmation paved the way for full Orthodox participation. But, argued the great ecumenical leader Lesslie Newbigin, it would have been better to say that no church is obliged to change as a *condition* of membership in the Council. Membership does not mean that churches enter the fellowship of a council agreeing about the nature of the church. To stop there, however, is to reduce the council to a debating society and implicitly endorse the present form of conciliar relationship as an adequate expression of Christian fellowship. "It is good," writes Newbigin, "that churches should be reassured in respect to any fear that they might surrender their convictions for the sake of some [hu]man-made

[24]Lukas Vischer, "Christian Councils—Instruments of Ecclesial Communion," in Kinnamon and Cope, 472.
[25]*Towards a Common Understanding,* para. 3.5.3.
[26]In Kinnamon and Cope, 465.

organization. But it is also good that they should be reminded that they might fall into the hands of the living God"[27]—and be changed.

It follows that councils of churches must be regarded as provisional, must always be prepared to die in order that fuller manifestations of communion may be born. They are steps toward deeper fellowship *as the church,* which is why councils dare not become service organizations aimed at self-perpetuation. "The worst thing that could happen to the Council," wrote Visser't Hooft in his *Memoirs,* "would be that it should come to be considered as just another cog in the ecclesiastical machinery."[28] Councils, through their programs and decision-making bodies, must always insist on the growing commitment of the member churches to one another. Otherwise, they can actually hinder the work of ecumenism. The WCC's Faith and Order Commission put this issue in the form of questions: "Do councils continue to serve the cause of unity, or do they rather institutionalize a limited degree of unity and perpetuate division? Do they serve to go on to the next step on the road, or do they give the churches a good conscience by leaving them at a stage where they are not quite divided but not yet united?"[29] Roman Catholic theologian Jean Tillard uses a more graphic analogy. Unless the aim is visible unity, he writes, councils run the risk of becoming like De Gaulle's description of the Vichy government: an institution whose sole result is "to make the shame of defeat acceptable."[30]

* * *

If I were to write a "basis" statement for a council of churches, drawing on the insights found in this chapter, what would it look like? That is a question I tried to answer in a book, *Councils of Churches and the Ecumenical Vision,* co-authored with Diane Kessler, executive director of the Massachusetts state council. I reproduce that suggested basis here as a way of summarizing the preceding argument:

> The Council of Churches is a fellowship of churches which, in response to the gospel as revealed in scripture, confess Jesus Christ as Savior and Lord. Relying upon the power of the Holy

---

[27]In Kinnamon and Cope, 470.

[28]Visser't Hooft, *Memoirs,* 345.

[29]*Sharing in One Hope: Reports and Documents from the 1978 Meeting of the Faith and Order Commission* (Geneva: WCC, 1978), 282.

[30]J. M. R. Tillard, "The Mission of Councils of Churches," *The Ecumenical Review* 45 (July 1993): 276.

Spirit, these churches covenant with one another to engage in common mission and to manifest ever more fully the unity of the church.

In affirming this covenant, our churches confess that apart from one another we are impoverished and repent of our frequent failure to make our own the joys and struggles of the other member communions. We recognize that membership in the Council entails the responsibility of bearing witness to the gospel as we have received it, but also the opportunity of being challenged and inspired by perspectives other than our own. We acknowledge that the Council is a forum in which dialogue about the nature and purpose of the church rightly takes place, a forum in which all members are responsible for speaking and hearing the truth in love. We also acknowledge that, while membership in the _____ Council of Churches does not necessarily imply full recognition of the other members as "church," it is based on the recognition of certain sacred bonds between us, including:

- proclamation through word and deed of the gospel, God's reconciling and redeeming love for all creation as revealed in Christ and recorded in scripture;

- incorporation into Christ through baptism [if all of the members practice baptism];

- worship through word and sacrament of the one God, Father, Son and Holy Spirit;

- ministries of service and witness in Christ's name.

These are significant signs of the oneness we already have as followers of Jesus Christ. We also recognize, however, that our life together as a council of churches, if it is led by the Spirit, can never be static. We pray that our relationships may deepen and expand toward the day when all Christians in this place visibly love one another, and all of God's children, even as Christ has loved us.[31]

---

[31]Kessler and Kinnamon, 26–27.

— 8 —

Unity in Christ

Why Interfaith Relations Are a Good but Different Thing

Several chapters in this book have dealt at length with significant changes in the ecumenical movement that took place in the 1960s. Some of these changes, such as the stronger emphasis on the unity and renewal of humankind, I obviously regard as positive—so long as this emphasis is not divorced from the movement's concern for the unity and renewal of the church. Some, such as the diminished focus on and leadership of the laity, I do not regard so positively.

This chapter will highlight another change of this period, one that is perhaps more seismic and controversial than any yet discussed: the emergence of interfaith dialogue (and, more generally, interfaith relations) as a distinctive item on the ecumenical agenda. In this case, I believe that there are important new insights to be affirmed, some of which are at odds with parts of the "classic" ecumenical vision. But, once again, the contemporary ecumenical movement is in danger of being impoverished, at least in my judgment, by losing touch with elements of its vision that are essential.

* * *

The ecumenical movement, from its inception, has been centered on Christ. The so-called Paris basis of the YMCA, adopted in 1855, speaks of seeking to unite young men who regard "Jesus Christ as their God and Savior according to the Holy Scriptures."[1] This language, which echoes Titus 2:13, was picked up by the early Faith and Order movement and eventually incorporated into the formal Basis of the World Council of Churches. Themes from WCC assemblies, at least through 1983, reaffirmed this christocentric focus: "Christ–The Hope of the World" (Evanston, 1954), "Jesus Christ–The Light of the World" (New Delhi, 1961), "Jesus Christ Frees and Unites" (Nairobi, 1975), "Jesus Christ– The Life of the World" (Vancouver, 1983).

I need quickly to add that the early movement was certainly trinitarian, though in a way that emphasized the particular Christian doctrines of incarnation and atonement ("Jesus Christ as God and Savior"). The following quotations–the first is from the Edinburgh conference on Faith and Order (1937), the second from Willem Visser't Hooft's book *The Pressure of Our Common Calling*–are representative:

> We are one in faith in our Lord Jesus Christ, the incarnate word of God. We are one in allegiance to him as head of the church, and as King of kings and Lord of lords. We are one in acknowledging that this allegiance takes precedence of any other allegiance that may make claims upon us. This unity does not consist in the agreement of our minds or the consent of our wills. It is founded on Jesus Christ himself, who lived and died and rose again to bring us to the Father, and who through the Holy Spirit dwells in his church.[2]

> The motivating force of the ecumenical movement is the rediscovery of the church as the church of God rooted in the work of Christ, the indispensable instrument for the fulfillment of the divine plan, existing essentially as one single people gathered by the Holy Spirit.[3]

---

[1]Ruth Rouse and Stephen Charles Neill, *The History of the Ecumenical Movement,* vol. 1 (Philadelphia: Westminster Press, 1967), 327.

[2]In Michael Kinnamon and Brian E. Cope, eds., *The Ecumenical Movement: An Anthology of Key Texts and Voices* (Geneva: WCC; Grand Rapids, Mich.: Eerdmans, 1997), 85.

[3]W. A. Visser't Hooft, *The Pressure of Our Common Calling* (Garden City, N.Y.: Doubleday, 1959), 13–14.

A trinitarian framework—"to the glory of the one God, Father, Son and Holy Spirit"—was explicitly added to the WCC Basis in 1961.[4]

It could have been otherwise. Visser't Hooft observed in several of his writings that the nascent ecumenical movement faced a decisive fork in the road in the late 1920s and early 1930s: "Would it move towards a Christ-centered ecumenism? Or towards an all-embracing union of religions?"[5] The latter option was highly appealing given the "internationalism" of the age and the obvious need for religious cooperation in the cause of peace. One expression of this was the Universal Religious Peace Conference of 1928, organized by a key figure in the Stockholm conference on Life and Work, Henry Atkinson. So prevalent was talk of interreligious cooperation that Pope Pius XI's 1928 encyclical *Mortalium Animos* condemned ecumenism as a movement based on "the erroneous view that all religions are more or less good and praiseworthy."[6]

In fact, however, the movement was taking the other fork. The church was involved in peacemaking and other international issues, ecumenical gatherings of the 1930s affirmed, because it followed the Prince of Peace whose sacrifice was decisive for all humanity. It was in living out its specific calling as the body of Christ that the Christian community could best serve a dangerously divided world. "We live at a time," said the Message from the 1937 Life and Work conference in Oxford, "when [hu]man kind is oppressed by perplexity and evil...Yet we do not take up our task as bewildered citizens of our several nations, asking if anywhere there is a clue to our problems; we take it up as Christians, to whom is committed 'the word of reconciliation,' that 'God was in Christ reconciling the world unto himself.'"[7]

Most explicit references to people of other faiths, in the years leading up to the founding of the World Council, came in the context of the International Missionary Council, whose chief aim was to pool resources and develop common strategies in order to "win the world for Christ." The IMC's Jerusalem meeting (1928) did talk of joining hands with other religious persons against the threat of secularism, symbolized especially by the Russian revolution, but such contact was still seen

---

[4]In Kinnamon and Cope, 469.

[5]W. A. Visser't Hooft, *Has the Ecumenical Movement a Future?* (Belfast, Ireland: Christian Journals Ltd., 1974), 56.

[6]See Rouse and Neill, 682.

[7]J. H. Oldham, *The Oxford Conference: Official Report* (Chicago: Willett, Clark, 1937), 45.

primarily as preparation for evangelism.[8] This perspective was most vigorously affirmed at the IMC's 1938 conference in Tambaram, India: "We see and readily recognize that in [non-Christian religions] are to be found values of deep religious experiences and great moral achievements. Yet we are bold enough to call [people] out from them to the feet of Christ. We do so because we believe that in him alone is the full salvation which [humanity] needs."[9]

According to Sri Lankan ecumenist Wesley Ariarajah, the first sign of transition to a new understanding came in 1956 when ecumenical study centers around the world were invited to participate in a project entitled "The Word of God and the Living Faiths of Men." This led some Christian leaders to ask, "How can we talk *about* people of other faiths unless we first talk *with* them?" And thus, writes Ariarajah, "the concept of 'dialogue' was born."[10] Behind it is a key methodological conviction: Other faiths should not be judged in the abstract but should be experienced through living encounter.

The first WCC assembly to speak about interfaith dialogue was New Delhi (1961). It was followed quickly by the Second Vatican Council, which contended in one of its "declarations": "All [people] form but one community. This is so because all stem from the one stock which God created to people the entire earth, and also because all share a common destiny, namely God."[11] Different religions, said the Catholic bishops, recognize God, and this recognition "results in a way of life that is imbued with a deep religious sense...The church, therefore, urges her sons [and daughters] to enter with prudence and charity in discussion and collaboration with members of other religions."[12] A Vatican Secretariat for Non-Christians was established by Pope Paul VI following the Council, and by 1971 the WCC had created its own office on Dialogue with People of Living Faiths and Ideologies, thus removing interfaith relations from the framework of mission and evangelism.

There are several obvious sociological reasons for this rapid shift of perspective. Religious diversity, always the experience of Christians in Asia and Africa, was increasingly characteristic of Europe and North America as well. Church leaders in the West were now aware that the

---

[8]Kinnamon and Cope, 394–95

[9]*The Authority of Faith: International Missionary Council Meeting at Tambaram*, vol. 1 (London: Oxford University Press, 1939), 200.

[10]S. Wesley Ariarajah, "The Ecumenical Impact of Inter-Religious Dialogue," *The Ecumenical Review* 49 (April 1997): 214.

[11]In Kinnamon and Cope, 399.

[12]Ibid.

spread of Western civilization, contrary to the expectations of previous generations, was not leading to the extinction of non-Christian religions. In fact, with the end of colonization, these faith communities were beginning to assert their own validity with growing zeal. Meanwhile, Christians outside the North Atlantic region were also finding their voice, and many of them were using it to encourage a more cooperative approach to other religions. Their primary agenda was often nation building and the struggle against oppression, activities that were, in many cases, directed against other Christians and undertaken alongside persons of other religions.

This is not to suggest that the ecumenical movement was suddenly of one mind about the topic! The 1975 WCC assembly in Nairobi, the first assembly with interfaith guests, was marked by open controversy.[13] How does dialogue avoid the danger of syncretism? Does dialogue undermine Christian mission? What about the uniqueness of God's revelation in Jesus Christ? Such questions are still not (and may never be) fully resolved, but there is now broad support, among those churches involved in ecumenical work, for eschewing triumphalist forms of evangelism and for working with others in the building of a better society. Books on ecumenism before 1970 rarely talked about interfaith dialogue; a decade later such discussion was nearly obligatory. Interfaith dialogues and activities can now be found in communities around the world. Interfaith events, such as the Parliament of Religions (1993 and 1999), with its attempt to produce a "global ethic," have generated considerable excitement in ecumenical circles. Many churches have expanded their ecumenical departments to include an interfaith desk, and numerous churches in Europe and North America have developed statements on interfaith relations.

What I want to stress, however, is that this new concern for interreligious dialogue has generally been understood, at least within ecumenical organizations, not as a challenge to but an outgrowth of the churches' confession of Jesus Christ. A good example is the document "Guidelines on Dialogue with People of Living Faiths and Ideologies," perhaps the most influential text produced by the WCC's dialogue office. According to the "Guidelines," interfaith dialogue is properly understood as "mutual witness," and, thus, the authors "feel able with integrity to commend the way of dialogue as one in which Jesus Christ is confessed

---

[13]See David M. Paton, *Breaking Barriers: Official Report of the Fifth Assembly of the World Council of Churches* (London: SPCK, 1976), 70–73.

in the world today."[14] The document includes this unambiguous confession:

> We are specifically disciples of Christ, but we refuse to limit him to the dimensions of our human understanding. In our relationships within the many human communities, we believe that we come to know Christ more fully through faith as Son of God and Savior of the world; we grow in his service within the world; and we rejoice in the hope he gives.[15]

The first director of the WCC's dialogue office, Indian scholar Stanley Samartha, was even more explicit. The following quotation is from his address to the World Council's Central Committee in 1971:

> The basis on which Christians enter into and continue their dialogue with others is their faith in Jesus Christ, the Son of God, who has become man on behalf of all people of all ages and of all cultures...It is christology, not "comparative religion," that is the basis of our concern. Our primary interest is not in "inter-religious conferences;" it is to be with Christ in his continuing work among people of all faiths and ideologies. Christ draws us out of our isolation into closer relationship with all.[16]

* * *

There is another, more recent development that must figure in our discussion, and that is the call for a "wider ecumenism." Raimon Panikkar has, for years, spoken of an "ecumenical ecumenism" that would move beyond "settling Christian family feuds" to a "multi-voiced dialogue" among religions.[17] Konrad Raiser has also raised the issue in his book *To Be the Church*.[18] The fullest challenge, however, has come from Wesley Ariarajah, a former deputy general secretary of the WCC. Ariarajah acknowledges that no one with even a cursory knowledge of the movement can accuse its pioneers of ignoring the *oikoumene*, the "whole inhabited earth" beyond the boundaries of the church. But

---

[14] In Kinnamon and Cope, 408.

[15] "Dialogue in Community," *The Ecumenical Review* 29 (July 1977): 260.

[16] S. J. Samartha, *Courage for Dialogue: Ecumenical Issues in Inter-Religious Relationships* (Geneva: WCC, 1981), 12.

[17] Raimon Panikkar, *The Intra-Religious Dialogue* (New York: Paulist Press, 1999), 104.

[18] Konrad Raiser, *To Be the Church: Challenges and Hopes for a New Millennium* (Geneva: WCC, 1997), chaps. 1 and 2.

"unless what is 'ecumenical' is not simply *about,* but in some measure *constitutes,* the whole inhabited earth, it has too little to say to, and much less to do with, the majority of the world's population. Hence the call for 'wider ecumenism.'"[19] This call, he argues, is not a loss of confidence in the gospel (as some have suggested) but a new "confidence in God," who intends unity and renewal for all the peoples of the earth. It is time for the church to grow beyond the focus on its own unity, its own mission and service *to* the world, and to locate itself more fully *in* the world. This, of course, would move interfaith relations from the margins to the center of the ecumenical agenda.

Ariarajah, for whom I have great respect, insists that "there is nothing in interfaith encounter which calls a halt to the search for Christian unity."[20] Indeed, he has personally demonstrated a capacity to care deeply about both the renewal of the church and the wider circle of interreligious dialogue. I am afraid, however, that this is not the case with some who now use the language or concept of wider ecumenism. Many of my seminary students, for example, regard Christian ecumenism as exclusivist and passé. They see it contrasted with interfaith relations and clearly prefer to devote their energies to the latter. Meanwhile, local councils of churches throughout the U.S. have "expanded" to include interfaith members. Diane Kessler, director of the Massachusetts Council of Churches, counts more than a dozen interfaith organizations in her state, most of them former councils of churches. When this happens, according to Kessler, a basic change in purpose often occurs, and "all efforts to heal the still considerable divisions among the Christian churches are lost."[21]

I need to make my own position clear. I believe that the ecumenical vision can be impoverished in two very different ways. On the one hand, it can be impoverished by minimizing the importance of interfaith dialogue and the lessons learned through it in recent years. Dialogue and cooperation with people of other religious traditions belong on the ecumenical agenda for several obvious reasons: (1) The movement is properly concerned with the problems and future of the *oikoumene.* How can Christians pursue peace or justice or ecological responsibility apart from neighbors of other faiths?! (2) Interfaith dialogue is something that

---

[19]S. Wesley Ariarajah, "Wider Ecumenism: A Threat or a Promise?" *The Ecumenical Review* 50 (July 1998): 328.

[20]Ariariajah, "Ecumenical Impact," 220.

[21]Diane C. Kessler, "New Angles in a Lively Debate: Should Ecumenical Organizations Be Christian or Interfaith?" *Mid-Stream* 32 (October 1993): 31, 32.

the churches properly do together. It makes little sense to talk about Buddhist-Methodist or Jewish-Presbyterian dialogue! Interfaith relations should force Christians to think *as Christians*–which is why such relations can provoke *ecumenical* advance. (3) The question of the place of other religions in God's plan of salvation is a topic of great controversy within Christianity and, thus, must be addressed ecumenically.

On the other hand, the vision is greatly impoverished if Christian ecumenism and interfaith relations are confused or collapsed, as if the latter were simply an expanded version of the former. Four observations may help to support this claim.

1. Christian ecumenism and interfaith relations have different goals, reflecting different theological foundations. Ecumenism, as I have argued throughout this book, is a renewal effort that seeks to express the communion *(koinonia)* that Christians have with one another through Christ in order to witness to the gospel and to participate in God's work of justice and reconciliation more faithfully and effectively. This communion–which, Christians confess, is a gift of God–is marked by a shared allegiance to Christ that (in theory) is more significant than any differences among us. The goal, in short, is life together so intense that the joys and sorrows of one become the joys and sorrows of all.

From a Christian perspective, interfaith relations also have a compelling theological foundation: humanity's common creation in the image of God. But this "ecumenical ecumenism," as Panikkar notes, "does not aim directly at unity but at understanding."[22] The basis is not shared confession but shared recognition of common humanity that moves us not to *koinonia* but to cooperative partnership on behalf of the human future. I do not mean to minimize this in the least. My point is not that intra-Christian ecumenism is "better" than interfaith relationships, but that they are different. As Kessler points out, interfaith organizations almost always (necessarily) focus on what religious bodies can *do* together, whereas councils of churches should also (primarily) be concerned with what Christians *are* together through Christ.[23]

2. There is great need–desperate need–for a movement that seeks deeper cooperation among religions; but there is *also* need–desperate need–for one that seeks to manifest the unity of the church. Of course, not everyone or even every member of the church cares that Christians are still divided at the Lord's table, that the array of denominations seems

---

[22]Panikkar, 108.
[23]Kessler, 33.

to deny the power of Christ to reconcile those who are different, that liberals and conservatives continue to pronounce anathemas (official and unofficial) on one another, that Christians go to war against one another without apparent thought to the *una sancta.* But it is hard to see how those who love the body of Christ can rest content with its present witness.

3. Most scholars on the subject now seem to affirm that dialogue in a pluralistic setting does not mean avoiding particular claims (e.g., that Jesus Christ is the Son of God). It means, rather, bringing such claims into conversation with other particularities (e.g., that Mohammed is the seal of the prophets). In this sense, fruitful interfaith dialogue presupposes ecumenical conversations aimed at clarifying the Christian confession.

4. Behind all of these arguments is my conviction that Christian claims *are true,* that God has acted in Christ and continues to act through the Spirit for the salvation of the world, that the church does have a story to tell to the nations. Raiser, Ariarajah, and Samartha all rightly deplore a "Christomonism" that "tends to regard Jesus Christ as 'the Christians' God' and makes it impossible to have any meaningful dialogue with neighbors of other faiths."[24] But this is, by no means, the same as a "Christocentrism" that confesses Jesus Christ as the Word made flesh "full of grace and truth" (John 1:14); the one in whom God was "reconciling the world to himself" (2 Corinthians 5:19); the one who, though in the form of God, "emptied himself...being born in human likeness," and suffered death for the sake of the world (Philippians 2:5–8). It is this confession, foundational for the Christian ecumenical movement, that constitutes part of the "mutual witness" we engage in with people of different faiths.

There are many Christian leaders who exemplify the perspective I have been trying to suggest in this chapter, but one I wish to name is Philip Potter, general secretary of the World Council of Churches during the transition to greater openness to neighbors of other faiths. Potter's book *Life in All Its Fullness,* a collection of speeches and writings from his years of leadership in the WCC, is suffused with biblically grounded faith in Christ. "The whole drama of salvation, our liberation, is centered in the disclosure of the reality of God in the man Jesus and in the overcoming of the offense [of sin] by those who accept him in faith. That recovery of the word for the church is what the modern movements of Christian renewal [including ecumenism] are seeking to

---

[24]Samartha, 96.

emphasize."[25] Potter is probably best known for his commitment to social justice and inclusivity, but he is also clear that faithfulness to the gospel means expressing in word and deed the given oneness of the church. Indeed, "to be indifferent to the unity of the church as the body of Christ is to be indifferent to Christ."[26]

At the same time, Potter leaves no doubt that interfaith dialogue is a complementary activity, an act of obedience to Christ and an expression of our faith in God, whose unsearchable riches come to us in unexpected places. The following passages give a flavor of his argument:

> [Interreligious dialogue] is an act of faith, a giving of the blessing, a sharing with the other of all that we have received from God in Christ. It is also the recognition that, in the inscrutable wisdom of God, the other has some blessing to bestow, some life and vitality from the depths of being. Christ is only betrayed when we deny ourselves of this outgoing, outpouring covenant blessing to the other and with the other.[27]

> Dialogue [with people of other religious traditions] is a form of existence, the form of the incarnate Lord as a servant living among human beings, open and vulnerable to them. It is the way of the cross.[28]

> We are to show to others [of whatever faith] the same profound respect and awe that we show to Christ. And with it must be the gentleness which is expressed in caring concern for the other— the willingness to receive as well as to give, to listen as well as to speak. It is this respect and caring, which Christ displayed to us and demands of us, that we must manifest to others.[29]

---

[25]Philip Potter, *Life in All Its Fullness* (Geneva: WCC, 1981), 10–11.
[26]Ibid., 37.
[27]Ibid., 50–51.
[28]Ibid., 81.
[29]Ibid., 163–64.

Conclusion

At the 1998 assembly of the World Council of Churches, the WCC's general secretary, Konrad Raiser, asked the question that is behind this book: "Do we have an ecumenical vision which could guide us as we move into the twenty-first century and which is compelling enough to inspire a new generation?"[1] This is a question heard often these days in ecumenical circles, and much of the discussion surrounds Raiser himself.

In his book *Ecumenism in Transition: A Paradigm Shift in the Ecumenical Movement?* Raiser repeats a familiar lament: The contemporary movement is marked by uncertainty, stagnation, and a loss of direction and vision. There is even little shared understanding of what is meant by the word *ecumenical*. However, the proper label for this state of affairs, as he sees it, is not "crisis" but "transition." "If one starts from this hypothesis of an incipient change in the basic intellectual frame of reference, then the crises in many areas appear in a different light. Then they are not so much signs of decline and disintegration but rather indications of an unconscious search"[2]–the search for a new paradigm.

Raiser identifies two previous paradigms that have shaped the development of modern ecumenism. The first initiatives for cooperation between the churches–or, at least, between Christians of different confessions–came in the late nineteenth century and were based on an assumed synthesis between Christianity and Western culture. The following statement by renowned political scientist Samuel Huntington puts the development of modern ecumenism in interesting (chilling) perspective: "By 1910 [the year of the Edinburgh World Missionary Conference, often referred to as the symbolic beginning of the ecumenical movement] the world was more one, politically and economically, than at any other time in human history."[3] Europe and its former

---

[1]Diane Kessler, ed., *Together on the Way: Official Report of the Eighth Assembly of the World Council of Churches* (Geneva: WCC, 1999), 99.

[2]Konrad Raiser, *Ecumenism in Transition: A Paradigm Shift in the Ecumenical Movement?* trans. Tony Coates (Geneva: WCC, 1991), 33.

[3]Samuel P. Huntington, *The Clash of Civilizations and the Remaking of World Order* (New York: Touchstone Books, 1996), 51.

colonies in North America controlled 84 percent of the earth's land surface, nearly 50 percent of its population, and roughly 70 percent of the world's economic output. It was indeed possible to envision human unity as a global Christian civilization.

All of this began to disintegrate, of course, with the First World War— in effect, a Christian civil war which pitted Protestant Britain, Catholic France, and Orthodox Russia against Protestant Germany, Catholic Austria, and Orthodox Bulgaria. The paradigm was further eroded by the Russian revolution, the increasing secularization of Western society, the economic crisis of the 1930s, the emergence of fascism in the heart of "Christian Europe," and the collapse of colonial rule, including an abrupt end to the most ambitious of all missionary enterprises–China.

The real vision of the modern ecumenical movement, as I understand it, grew in the midst of these events, and no doubt bears their stamp. Lesslie Newbigin put it simply: "The WCC was born in the death-throes of 'Christendom.'"[4] It cut its theological teeth on the German Church Struggle, the horrifying trauma of World War II, and the movements for independence that accompanied or stemmed from this conflict.

The paradigm that emerged Raiser calls "christocentric universalism," borrowing a phrase from Willem Visser't Hooft, who was its chief exponent. At the center of God's plan of salvation is God's self-revelation in Jesus Christ, with "the church as the chosen instrument of the world-embracing saving work of Christ."[5] To put it another way, the church proclaims to the world that it stands under the lordship of Christ, and it demonstrates the credibility of that claim by its visible unity as well as its ministry of word and deed throughout the *oikoumene*–a vision that brings together unity, service, and mission. The following passage from *No Other Name*, a book Raiser quotes at length, is typical of Visser't Hooft's thought.

> New Testament universalism is…characterized by the fact that in it the central figure, the body which he creates and the humanity for whom he has given his life, belong together and are inseparable. Uniqueness [of Christ], unity and universality are all indispensable and mutually interdependent. There is no universality if there is no unique event. But the unique event is not realized in its significance where there is no movement forward and outward toward universality. And the link between

---

[4]Lesslie Newbigin, "A Missionary's Dream ," *The Ecumenical Review* 42 (January 1991): 4.
[5]W. A. Visser't Hooft, quoted in Raiser, 37.

the two is in the body which in its unity, transcending all divisions, is the first fruit of the new humanity...The ecumenical movement of our time is an attempt to realize this specific Christian universalism.[6]

This paradigm, as Raiser observes, gave the movement momentum and direction after the Second World War, provided a vision of the church's nature and purpose in the aftermath of Christendom, and was effective both in challenging the "cultural religion" of Western Protestantism and in opposing Nazis. In his judgment, however, this christocentric universalism has lost its compelling power as a result of several historical developments, including the growth of religious pluralism in traditionally Christian societies that challenges christocentric language, the rise of ecological awareness that challenges the focus on human history, and the astonishing diversity of culture and confession in the church that challenges notions of unity as consensus. The old paradigm, he argues, is unhistorical and dogmatic. That is, it makes exaggerated claims for the church and plays down the "messiness" of actual history; it judges history on the basis of doctrinal claims about the church and the world rather than on the concrete experience of suffering and relationships.

> The "*oikoumene*"...is not a description of a given state of affairs. It is not a matter of structures, but of dynamic, real relationships. When we say, "*oikoumene*," we are not referring to a global abstraction, such as "one world," the "whole human race," or "one united world church." What we are speaking of are the actual and at the same time endangered connections and relationships between churches, between cultures, between people and human societies in their infinite variety, and between the world of humankind and creation as a whole.[7]

The new paradigm that Raiser sees emerging has three main features: (1) a more trinitarian understanding that stresses God's universal covenant, the interrelatedness of all humanity in God's coming reign; (2) a central focus on the whole of creation, understood as a web of reciprocal relationships; and (3) an understanding of church that minimizes agreement in faith and emphasizes the fellowship *(koinonia)*

---

[6]W. A. Visser't Hooft, *No Other Name* (London: SCM Press, 1963), 102.
[7]Raiser, 86.

of those who are different.[8] His controlling image, borrowed from Philip Potter, is the "household *(oikos)* of God," characterized by dialogue, hospitality, and acts of sharing and solidarity.[9]

As Raiser describes them, the three paradigms are reminiscent of the "exclusivist-inclusivist-pluralist" typology often used to describe the various Christian approaches to interfaith relations: (1) an international order based on Christian values in which the church is all in all; (2) Christ as the center of universal history, with the church as the primary instrument of God's saving mission; and (3) the church as one community among many in God's *oikoumene.*

Raiser's depiction of ecumenism in transition has been received by many with real appreciation (to which I will return), but has also been vigorously attacked. Geoffrey Wainwright argues that the Uppsala Assembly, a positive turning point in Raiser's estimation, is where the WCC actually went astray, losing touch with its primary concern for the church and its focus on Christ. Raiser, as he sees it, continues down this wrong fork in the road.[10] Jeffrey Gros, writing from a Catholic perspective, contends that Raiser truncates the ecumenical vision by failing to hold in tension the struggle to realize the visible unity of the church as a community of shared faith and eucharistic fellowship and the struggle to realize a human community of justice and peace. "His book can be considered a polemic against the wholeness advocated by the WCC."[11] Lesslie Newbigin suggests that Raiser's thesis ignores the missionary movement and, thus, radically distorts ecumenical history.[12]

*   *   *

Given my concern for church unity and my appreciation for Visser't Hooft, it might seem as if this book is intended as a refutation of Raiser. That, however, would not really be accurate.

I deeply appreciate, for example, Raiser's reminder that vision can never be static but must always be rethought and restated in light of new circumstances. As I see it, the ecumenical movement is still thinking

---

[8]Ibid., 79.

[9]Ibid., 102–11.

[10]Geoffrey Wainwright, review of *Ecumenism in Transition* in *Mid-Stream* 31 (April 1992): 169–73.

[11]Jeffrey Gros, review of *Ecumenism in Transition* in *The Christian Century* (July 29–August 5, 1992): 718.

[12]Lesslie Newbigin, review of *Ecumenism in Transition* in *One in Christ* 29, no. 3 (1993): 274–75.

through the implications of the incredible transitions that took place in the 1960s and early 1970s:

- The Roman Catholic Church and the Orthodox churches made what each called an "unequivocal" commitment to the cause of Christian unity, thus making the ecumenical movement far more theologically inclusive.

- As nations in Africa, Asia, Latin America, and the Pacific gained their independence following the demise of colonialism, churches in these regions claimed a new selfhood and began to assert their priorities for the ecumenical movement, thus making it far more culturally inclusive.

- Woman, racial minorities, and other formerly marginalized groups began to claim their rightful place in church leadership, thus making the movement more humanly inclusive.

- People of other faiths appeared on the theological radar screen, thus making the ecumenical agenda more religiously inclusive.

- Concern for creation (ecology) surfaced as a mission priority, thus making the movement's agenda more inclusive—period!

All these changes are helpfully examined in *Ecumenism in Transition*.

Raiser also seems to be reconsidering what he means by paradigm shift. In the "Postscript" to the English edition of *Ecumenism in Transition,* he denies that his intent is to proclaim a new paradigm, a new vision in place of the old.

> Even less am I suggesting a simple break of continuity in the process of transition from the "old" to the "new." In fact, the notion of "paradigm shift" implies that any new frame of orientation can claim validity only to the extent that it succeeds in preserving and integrating the truth contained in earlier perceptions. Therefore, it is not a matter of replacing the "christocentric universalism" of the past, but of integrating it into a more comprehensive perspective that meets the challenges and contradictions that have arisen.[13]

Raiser put it this way in his address to the Harare Assembly:

---
[13]Raiser, 122.

It is not so much the central core of the vision itself which is at stake. The biblical symbols of the reign of God, of the fullness of life in the presence of God, of a new heaven and earth established on right relationships, the bringing together of all things into unity in Christ—these constitute the source of inspiration for our hopes and visions. The challenge to us here is rather to find a language in which to interpret and explicate these biblical images for the generations of today and tomorrow, that they might be equipped to respond to the ecumenical calling with the same conviction as did those generations who prepared the way.[14]

There are, however, obvious points at which we differ. In my judgment, Raiser still asserts too much discontinuity with the past. Trinitarianism, for example, is not an alternative to christocentrism. Christians have generally argued that the doctrine of the trinity is the context for any theologically sound understanding of Christ. We can affirm Christ as the center of our distinctive witness and the source of our distinctive community without in the least denying the importance of a full trinitarian understanding of God (and thus of God's presence throughout creation).

It is also my judgment that Raiser undervalues the significance of the church as a sign and instrument of God's reconciling mission. And as a result, he undervalues theological dialogue, often associated with Faith and Order, aimed at realizing the church's visible unity. Raiser sees dialogue as an end in itself, a "sharing of life,"[15] rather than an expression of the mutual correction that builds up the body of Christ. It is probably not surprising that the three reviewers, referred to above, charge him with failing to integrate the various streams of ecumenism, and even of exacerbating the tension between the concern for unity in faith and the concern for social justice through our mission in the world.

* * *

Much of the argument in this book has been negative—what the vision is not.

---

[14]In Kessler, 101.
[15]Raiser, 82–83, 106–7.

- The ecumenical vision insists that God has acted in Christ to bind all who follow him into one body, but we too often speak as if fellowship were our creation.

- The ecumenical vision insists that the church is renewed when Christians who are different share gifts with one another, but we speak more of tolerance and cooperation that leave intact the way we are.

- The ecumenical vision insists on the integration of church unity, social justice, and common witness, but we too often play these off against one another.

- The ecumenical vision insists that the church's given unity is wondrously diverse, but we too often speak of uniting our diversities.

- The ecumenical vision insists that unity and renewal are rooted in repentance for the ways Christians have offended against God and one another, but we too often speak of growth without repentance or conversion.

- The ecumenical vision has often been carried by laypersons who protest the way the church has denied its true nature and mandate, but we too often leave ecumenism to specialists to do on our behalf.

- The ecumenical vision understands councils of churches to be fellowships or communities of the churches themselves, but we too often regard councils as structures alongside or over against the churches.

- The ecumenical vision, while ultimately concerned with the whole of God's creation, is particularly concerned with the community of Christ's followers; but we are in danger of collapsing or confusing Christian ecumenism and interfaith relations.

Now it is time to state my own understanding of the vision in positive terms. I have long thought that one of the best short statements of the ecumenical vision is the theme from the WCC's Nairobi Assembly: "Jesus Christ Frees and Unites." This, of course, is a shorthand way of saying "God who was in Christ and who is continually present through the Holy Spirit frees and unites." The author of all true freedom and unity is God, the One who made the world and everything in it, the One in whom all persons live and move and have their being, the One who has not been left without a witness in all the nations. I want to unpack the five words of this theme by making six observations:

1. To say that Jesus Christ frees and unites not only names good news but also the bad news of our human condition. Human beings are in bondage, both to the power of sin and to the pharaohs of every age. But we are also fragmented, alienated from God, from neighbor, even from ourselves.

None of this will come as a surprise to anyone who has lived a year or two or read from almost any book of the Bible. What makes the ecumenical vision noteworthy, however, is the insistence that these go together; what makes the movement profound is its refusal to address only half of the human condition. Yes, previous generations of ecumenists tended to stress unity more than liberation, while today we tend to hear far more about the problem of oppression than the problem of fragmentation. But, at its best, the ecumenical movement has said both. Our gravest problems as a species include South Africa *and* Yugoslavia, loss of liberty *and* loss of community, racism *and* narcissistic individualism. We desperately need a savior who frees *and* unites.

2. The assembly might have said, "We are called by Jesus Christ to free and unite"—but that is a second step. The first thing Christians affirm is that freedom and unity, however they are understood, are gifts. "For freedom Christ has set us free. Stand firm, therefore, and do not submit again to a yoke of slavery" (Galatians 5:1). Make "every effort to maintain the unity of Spirit in the bond of peace. [For] there is one body...one Lord, one faith, one baptism, one God...of all" (Ephesians 4:3–6). Whenever Christians live and act together in defiance of the world's walls of hostility, it is not our achievement that we celebrate, but God's gift for which we give thanks.

What a difference this makes! If it is *our* unity, then we will almost certainly seek community with those who are like us, with people of whom we approve. But if unity is understood as a gift, then we are free to recognize how we are linked in community (in Christ) with persons we would likely ignore or avoid—which is part of our liberation.

Now, however, we are ready for that second step. Whenever Christians say "Jesus Christ does this or that," it is, in effect, a statement of our own agenda as the church. If Jesus Christ frees and unites, then we who confess to be his body must be free-ers and uniters ("ambassadors of reconciliation") *and* must live in a way that demonstrates both

freedom and unity. Otherwise, the message is made incredible by the
non-credibility of the messengers. I suspect that most of us would have
a tough time separating Marxism from the activities of Marxists or
distinguishing Rastafarianism from the actions and appearance of
Rastafarians. Why should we expect the society around us to distinguish
the gospel of Jesus Christ from the actions and appearance of those who
ostensibly define themselves by his name? We desperately need a
reformation, a renewal movement, that calls us back to this essential
truth.

3. This theme from the 1975 assembly in Nairobi, by holding
together freedom and unity, also points to the integration of Faith and
Order and Life and Work. Several observations may help make this
point. It is important to remember that freedom and unity go together
in *any* rendering of the gospel. At the most basic level, it is surely fear–
fear of others, fear of other*ness*–that keeps us from receiving God's gift
of community. But countless Christians have testified that knowledge
of God's gracious acceptance frees us from this cramped life of self-
confirmation, frees us to live no longer for ourselves or by ourselves–
but *for* Christ and *in* the community of his disciples.

At another level, Christians are surely divided as much by racism
and poverty and violence as by different theologies of the sacraments
or different understandings of authority–or, to say it better, such matters
are inseparable. Only a church that cares passionately for freedom can
speak authentically of unity; and only a church in which people of
different races live together, only a church which refuses in its own life
to endorse the obscene disparity between rich and poor, can work
authentically for freedom.

Let me put it more polemically. The search for church unity, as I
noted in chapter 3, can end up bolstering old patterns of domination
unless constantly coupled with a commitment to just, free relationships.
But the justice God wills is not merely the co-existence of separate groups
but a new community in which those who have been excluded and beaten
down find a place. Just as freedom is the criterion of authentic unity,
so unity is the mark of authentic freedom.

Holding these in a single vision is very difficult. Perhaps the hardest
of all ecumenical questions is this: Can there be unity as long as the
church includes both oppressed and oppressors? The moderator of the
WCC's Central Committee at the time of the Nairobi Assembly was
the great Indian theologian M. M. Thomas. The problem with this
question about oppressors and oppressed, said Thomas,

is that the lines are always more blurred than that. When compared to the West, I am a victim; when compared to the poor of India, I am a victimizer. Beyond that, the question overlooks the reality of divine forgiveness, which enables the oppressed to trust and the oppressor to repent, [and which] is always breaking in and transforming the conditions of our world.[16]

The idea that Jesus Christ frees and unites should warn us against a "cheap unity" that would avoid morally contested issues because they could be disruptive. The ecumenical vision is not served by cobbling together denominations with a minimum of change, nor is it served by occasional cooperation interspersed with long periods of benign neglect. We are talking about fellowship so intimate that the disparagement of every black Christian diminishes white members of the church, a community so intense that bombs dropped on Baghdad cause North Americans to suffer.

4. All that I have argued so far underscores how crucial repentance is to this ecumenical vision. No one has said this better than Robert McAfee Brown in his address at the Nairobi Assembly. The proper formulation of our theme, argued Brown, is "Jesus Christ Frees, Unites, *and Divides.*" Or, since division can't be the first or last word for Christians, "Jesus Christ Frees, Divides, and Unites"—in that order. We are so often the source of one another's bondage. If our response to the liberating gospel is not repentance and change, then, said Brown, we still will be separated from our neighbors because of our own sin. It is the recognition of our culpability that makes it possible to receive the gift of unity.[17]

Ecumenism is also a movement of repentance, because the way we live as church is such a visible denial of the word we proclaim. What does it mean to say "Jesus Christ unites" in Northern Ireland or in the United States, with our array of denominations tailored to a consumerist society? What does it mean to say "Jesus Christ frees" in Rwanda (the African nation with the highest percentage of Christians) or in the United States, where the churches have long confused the gospel with the "American way of life"? Such claims must be made with humility if they are to be made at all. This, I take it, is why the bishops at the

---

[16]M. M. Thomas, *Towards a Theology of Contemporary Ecumenism* (Madras: CLS, 1978), 261–62.

[17]Brown's address is summarized in David M. Paton, ed., *Breaking Barriers: Official Report of the Fifth Assembly of the World Council of Churches* (London: SPCK, 1976), 12–13.

Second Vatican Council said there can be no ecumenism worthy of the name without interior conversion.

5. The dialectic of freedom and unity also helps define the nature of Christian communion—which is another way of saying that the fellowship of the church, the unity that Christ gives, is not uniform or coercive. Paul tries to express this by using the metaphor of a human body. Hidden in this image of interdependence is the miracle of the gospel. We who are different from one another, often so different that the world sees us as enemies, now freely acknowledge that we are nothing less than sisters and brothers in one family for no other reason than that we know ourselves to be the equally undeserving recipients of God's freely given grace. Diversity-in-communion is at the heart of our witness.

6. The theme might have read, "Jesus Christ Freed and United," but that would not do justice to the ongoing character of these gifts. Christians are those who remember what God has done, celebrate what God continues to do, and anticipate what God will do. Yes, Jesus Christ frees and unites here and now. But we also long for God's promised future when *all* creation will be freed from bondage and *no* person will labor in vain or bear children for calamity, for *all* will live in harmony on God's holy mountain. I care deeply about the church as a sign and instrument of God's future, but, as biblical scholars often point out, there is no church in the vision of Revelation 21. We used to say that the ecumenical movement took its marching orders from John 17 (the oneness of Jesus' disciples); but the passage I see quoted most often these days is from the first chapter of Ephesians: God's "plan for the fullness of time, to gather up [to reconcile] all things in him, things in heaven and things on earth" (v. 10). If renewal of the church is our *ultimate* goal, then we have missed the ecumenical (the *oikoumene*-centered) vision set forth in scripture.

This idea that unity, like freedom, is both a gift and a promise is also crucial because what we call unity is always partial and sometimes oppressive this side of the reign of God. Thus, there are times when Christians must disrupt our partial, temporary "unities" in order to live more fully that which God has given and promised. M. M. Thomas put it this way in his address at Nairobi: Christ "shatters every unity which turns into bondage…he makes men and women free to establish a more mature unity, only to break *it* when it too turns into bondage."[18] It is another way of saying that we follow a Savior who frees and unites.

---

[18]Thomas, 316.

Appendices

A Brief History of the Ecumenical Movement

The term *ecumenical movement* is generally used to designate those activities and organizations aimed at promoting common service, witness, and worship among now-divided Christian churches, thus making visible their God-given unity as the body of Christ. The movement has a great many manifestations. When representatives of separated churches attempt to heal theological differences dating back to the Reformation or before, their dialogues are part of the ecumenical movement. When denominations come together through councils of churches for disaster relief or advocacy on behalf of the poor, such shared activity is part of the ecumenical movement. When Christians of different church traditions join with one another to develop food pantries or celebrate the Week of Prayer for Christian Unity in their local churches, that, too, is part of the ecumenical movement.

The noun *ecumenism* and the adjective *ecumenical* are derived from the Greek word *oikoumene,* which is used in the New Testament to mean the Roman Empire or, simply, the whole inhabited earth. Gradually, the term came to refer to the whole church and to the whole faith of the church (as opposed to that which is partial or divisive). It is appropriate, therefore, that the word would eventually be associated with this modern movement, whose focus is the church's unity and universal mission.

In the nineteenth century, individual Christians began to work together, beyond the boundaries of their churches, through such organizations as the YMCA and YWCA, the Student Christian Movement, the World Sunday School Convention, and numerous mission and Bible societies. The beginning of the ecumenical movement, however, is usually identified with a world mission conference held in Edinburgh, Scotland, in 1910. That conference inspired three streams of ecumenical activity that reflect the movement's continuing priorities:

- Life and Work is that part of the movement concerned with fostering a common Christian response to such things as war, poverty, oppression, and natural calamity. Two early conferences of Life and Work–Stockholm (1925) and Oxford (1937)–are cited numerous times in the pages of this book.

- Faith and Order is that part of the movement concerned with overcoming doctrinal barriers to the visible unity of the church (e.g., disagreements over sacraments, ministry, and church authority). Participants in a series of Faith and Order conferences–Lausanne (1927), Edinburgh (1937), Lund (1952), Montreal (1963), and Santiago de Compostela (1993)––have also attempted to define the nature of Christian unity and to clarify its relationship to the wider context of human reconciliation.

- The International Missionary Council (IMC) had as its goal the promotion of a more cooperative approach to evangelism and a shared understanding of Christian mission. Reports from several international meetings of the IMC–Jerusalem (1928), Tambaram, India (1938), and Willingen, West Germany (1952)–are also cited in this volume.

By 1938, leaders of Faith and Order and Life and Work had determined that their efforts belonged together, a key insight in the development of what I am calling the *ecumenical vision*. This decision led to the formation of the WCC ten years later, and thirteen years after that, the IMC joined the Council. The WCC is not a central coordinating office for the ecumenical movement. It is, however, the movement's most prominent international organization and, as such, is referred to frequently in the argument of this book. In 2001, the WCC had 342 member churches (e.g., the Evangelical Lutheran Church in America or the Russian Orthodox Church), representing about a half billion Christians in 120 countries.

Guidance for the work of the World Council is provided by an assembly of delegates from the member churches that meets every seven or eight years in different parts of the world. Reports from these assemblies (listed below) are an invaluable resource for understanding the vision of this movement:

First Assembly	(Amsterdam, 1948)
Second Assembly	(Evanston, 1954)

Third Assembly	(New Delhi, 1961)
Fourth Assembly	(Uppsala, 1968)
Fifth Assembly	(Nairobi, 1975)
Sixth Assembly	(Vancouver, 1983)
Seventh Assembly	(Canberra, 1991)
Eighth Assembly	(Harare, 1998)

Since 1948, Faith and Order has continued its distinctive work as a commission of the WCC. Documents produced by the Faith and Order Commission—including the widely acclaimed text *Baptism, Eucharist, and Ministry*—figure prominently in my argument. The agenda of Life and Work is harder to trace since it was picked up by several WCC departments, but several international meetings—including the World Conference on Church and Society (Geneva, 1966), the World Conference on "faith, science and the future" (MIT, 1979), and the World Convocation on Justice, Peace, and the Integrity of Creation (Seoul, 1990)—stand in this stream of the movement. The IMC, when it merged with the World Council of Churches, became the Council's Commission on World Mission and Evangelism (CWME). Periodic CWME assemblies—Mexico City (1963), Bangkok (1973), Melbourne (1980), San Antonio (1989), and San Salvador (1996)—also contribute to our understanding of the ecumenical vision.

Creation of the WCC encouraged the birth of church councils in nearly every country and in thousands of local settings. Councils of churches play such a crucial role in the ecumenical movement that one entire chapter of this book is devoted to their nature and purpose.

It is important to stress that the ecumenical movement is by no means an intra-Protestant affair. As early as 1920, the Patriarch of Constantinople (also known as the Ecumenical Patriarch), spiritual leader of Eastern Orthodox Christianity, issued an encyclical calling for better relations among Christians and for the establishment of a "league between the churches." Several Orthodox churches were founding members of the WCC in 1948, and the remainder of the Orthodox world, both Eastern Orthodox and Oriental Orthodox, joined the Council in the early 1960s (though two churches have subsequently withdrawn their membership). Orthodox churches are also extensively involved in what are known as bilateral (two-party) theological dialogues, several of which are referred to in this book.

Until the 1950s, the Roman Catholic Church contended, through official pronouncements, that unity could only happen when non-Catholics "return to the one true church," and it thus forbade its members to participate in ecumenical dialogues or conferences. This changed dramatically, however, when in 1962 Pope John XXIII convened what is known as the Second Vatican Council (or Vatican II). The twenty-five hundred Catholic bishops who attended the sessions of Vatican II issued, among other documents, a *Decree on Ecumenism,* which spoke of all baptized Christians as sisters and brothers, deplored the sins against unity committed over the centuries by Catholics and Protestants alike, and called on "the Catholic faithful...to take an active and intelligent part in the work of ecumenism."

Since that time, the Catholic Church has become a major participant in the ecumenical movement–locally, nationally, and globally. A department of the Vatican, the Pontifical Council for Promoting Christian Unity, helps coordinate and encourage these efforts. Although not a member of the WCC, the Roman Catholic Church works closely with the Council on numerous projects, including the Week of Prayer for Christian Unity, and sends official participants to the WCC's major conferences and assemblies. A 1995 encyclical by Pope John Paul II, *Ut Unum Sint,* is one of the most significant ecumenical texts of recent years.[1]

---

[1]For a good short introduction to the history of the ecumenical movement, see Jeffrey Gros, Eamon McManus, and Ann Riggs, *Introduction to Ecumenism* (New York: Paulist Press, 1998), chap. 1. For more detailed information, see Michael Kinnamon and Brian E. Cope, eds., *The Ecumenical Movement: An Anthology of Key Texts and Voices* (Geneva: WCC; Grand Rapids, Mich.: Eerdmans, 1997); Ruth Rouse and Stephen Neill, eds., *A History of the Ecumenical Movement 1517–1948* (Philadelphia: Westminster Press, 1954); and Harold Fey, ed., *A History of the Ecumenical Movement 1948–1968* (Geneva: WCC, 1970). A third volume in this history series is forthcoming.

Willem Visser't Hooft called this encyclical, drafted by the holy synod of the Church of Constantinople, "an initiative which was without precedent in church history."[1] Although it generated little immediate response, this brief statement represents the first step toward formation of the World Council of Churches.

Unto the Churches of Christ Everywhere
Encyclical of the Ecumenical Patriarchate, 1920

"Love one another earnestly from the heart" (1 Pet. 1:22)

Our own church holds that rapprochement between the various Christian churches and fellowship between them is not excluded by the doctrinal differences which exist between them. In our opinion such a rapprochement is highly desirable and necessary. It would be useful in many ways for the real interest of each particular church and of the whole Christian body, and also for the preparation and advancement of that blessed union which will be completed in the future in accordance with the will of God. We therefore consider that the present time is most favourable for bringing forward this important question and studying it together.

Even if in this case, owing to antiquated prejudices, practices or pretensions, the difficulties which have so often jeopardized attempts at reunion in the past may arise or be brought up, nevertheless, in our view, since we are concerned at this initial stage only with contacts and rapprochement, these difficulties are of less importance. If there is "good will and intention," they cannot and should not create an invincible and insuperable obstacle.

---

[1]W. A. Visser't Hooft, *The Genesis and Formation of the WCC* (Geneva: WCC, 1982), 94–97.

Wherefore, considering such an endeavour to be both possible and timely, especially in view of the hopeful establishment of the League of Nations; we venture to express below in brief our thoughts and our opinion regarding the way in which we understand this rapprochement and contact and how we consider it to be realizable; we earnestly ask and invite the judgment and the opinion of the other sister churches in the East and of the venerable Christian churches in the West and everywhere in the world.

We believe that the two following measures would greatly contribute to the rapprochement which is so much to be desired and which would be so useful, and we believe that they would be both successful and fruitful:

First, we consider as necessary and indispensable the removal and abolition of all the mutual mistrust and bitterness between the different churches which arise from the tendency of some of them to entice and proselytize adherents of other confessions. For nobody ignores what is unfortunately happening today in many places, disturbing the internal peace of the churches, especially in the East. So many troubles and sufferings are caused by other Christians and great hatred and enmity are aroused, with such insignificant results, by this tendency of some to proselytize and entice the followers of other Christian confessions.

After this essential re-establishment of sincerity and confidence between the churches, we consider,

Secondly, that above all, love should be rekindled and strengthened among the churches, so that they should no more consider one another as strangers and foreigners, but as relatives, and as being a part of the household of Christ and "fellow heirs, members of the same body and partakers of the promise of God in Christ" (Eph. 3:6).

For if the different churches are inspired by love, and place it before everything else in their judgments of others and their relationships with them, instead of increasing and widening the existing dissensions, they should be enabled to reduce and diminish them. By stirring up a right brotherly interest in the condition, the wellbeing and stability of the other churches; by readiness to take an interest in what is happening in those churches and to obtain a better knowledge of them, and by willingness to offer mutual aid and help, many good things will be achieved for the glory and the benefit both of themselves and of the Christian body. In our opinion, such a friendship and kindly disposition towards each other can be shown and demonstrated particularly in the following ways:

a) By the acceptance of a uniform calendar for the celebration of the great Christian feasts at the same time by all the churches.

b) By the exchange of brotherly letters, on the occasion of the great feasts of the churches' year as is customary, and on other exceptional occasions.

c) By close relationships between the representatives of all churches wherever they may be.

d) By relationships between the theological schools and the professors of theology; by the exchange of theological and ecclesiastical reviews, and of other works published in each church.

e) By exchanging students for further training between the seminaries of the different churches.

f) By convoking pan-Christian conferences in order to examine questions of common interest to all the churches.

g) By impartial and deeper historical study of doctrinal differences both by the seminaries and in books.

h) By mutual respect for the customs and practices in different churches.

i) By allowing each other the use of chapels and cemeteries for the funerals and burials of believers of other confessions dying in foreign lands.

j) By the settlement of the question of mixed marriages between the confessions.

k) Lastly, by wholehearted mutual assistance for the churches in their endeavours for religious advancement, charity and so on.

Such a sincere and close contact between the churches will be all the more useful and profitable for the whole body of the Church, because manifold dangers threaten not only particular churches, but all of them. These dangers attack the very foundations of the Christian faith and the essence of Christian life and society. For the terrible world war which has just finished brought to light many unhealthy symptoms in the life of the Christian peoples, and often revealed great lack of respect even for the elementary principles of justice and charity. Thus it worsened already existing wounds and opened other new ones of a more material kind, which demand the attention and care of all the churches. Alcoholism, which is increasing daily; the increase of unnecessary luxury under the pretext of bettering life and enjoying it; the voluptuousness and lust hardly covered by the cloak of freedom and emancipation of the flesh; the prevailing unchecked licentiousness and indecency in literature, painting, the theatre, and in music, under the respectable name of the development of good taste and cultivation of fine art; the deification of wealth and the contempt of higher ideals; all these and the like, as they threaten the very essence of Christian societies, are also timely topics requiring and indeed necessitating common study and cooperation by the Christian churches.

Finally, it is the duty of the churches which bear the sacred name of Christ not to forget or neglect any longer hisnew and great commandment of love. Nor should they continue to fall piteously behind the political authorities, who, truly applying the spirit of the Gospel and the teaching of Christ, have under happy auspices already set up the so-called League of Nations in order to defend justice and cultivate charity and agreement between the nations.

For all these reasons, being ourselves convinced of the necessity for establishing a contact and league (fellowship) between the churches and believing that the other churches share our conviction as stated above, at least as a beginning we request each one of them to send us in reply a statement of its own judgment and opinion on this matter so that, common agreement or resolution having been reached, we may proceed together to its realization, and thus "speaking the truth in love, may grow up into him in all things, which is the head, even Christ; from whom the whole body fitly joined together and compacted by that which every joint supplieth, according to the effectual working in the measure of every part, maketh increase of the body unto the edifying of itself in love" (Eph. 4:15–16).

In the Patriarchate of Constantinople
in the month of January in the year of grace 1920

A Message from the Oxford Conference
to the Christian Churches

The Delegates to the World Conference on Church, Community and State, assembled at Oxford from July 12 to 26, 1937, send at the close of their deliberations the following message to the Churches of Christ throughout the world:—

In the name of Christ, greetings.

We meet at a time when mankind is oppressed with perplexity and fear. Men are burdened with evils almost insupportable and with problems apparently insoluble. Even in countries which are at peace unemployment and malnutrition sap men's strength of body, mind and spirit. In other countries war does its "devil's work," and threatens to overwhelm us all in its limitless catastrophe.

Yet we do not take up our task as bewildered citizens of our several nations, asking if anywhere there is a clue to our problems; we take it up as Christians, to whom is committed "the word of reconciliation," that "God was in Christ reconciling the world unto himself."

The first duty of the church, and its greatest service to the world, is that it be in very deed the church—confessing the true faith, committed to the fulfillment of the will of Christ, its only Lord, and united in him in a fellowship of love and service.

We do not call the world to be like ourselves, for we are already too like the world. Only as we ourselves repent, both as individuals and as corporate bodies, can the church call men to repentance. The call to ourselves and to the world is to Christ.

Despite our unfaithfulness God has done great things through his church. One of the greatest is this, that, not-withstanding the tragedy of our divisions and our inability in many important matters to speak with a united voice, there exists an actual world-fellowship. Our unity in Christ is not a theme for aspiration; it is an experienced fact. We can speak of it with boldness because our conference is an illustration of it.

131

We are drawn from many nations and from many different communions, from churches with centuries of history behind them and from the younger churches whose story covers but a few decades; but we are one in Christ.

The unity of this fellowship is not built up from its constituent parts, like a federation of different states. It consists in the sovereignty and redeeming acts of its one Lord. The source of unity is not the consenting movement of men's wills; it is Jesus Christ whose one life flows through the body and subdues the many wills to his.

The Christian sees distinctions of race as part of God's purpose to enrich mankind with a diversity of gifts. Against racial pride or race antagonism the church must set its face implacably as rebellion against God. Especially in its own life and worship there can be no place for barriers because of race or color. Similarly the Christian accepts national communities as part of God's purpose to enrich and diversify human life. Every man is called of God to serve his fellows in the community to which he belongs. But national egotism tending to the suppression of other nationalities or of minorities is, no less than individual egotism, a sin against the Creator of all peoples and races. The deification of nation, race or class, or of political or cultural ideals, is idolatry, and can lead only to increasing division and disaster.

On every side we see men seeking for a life of fellowship in which they experience their dependence on one another. But because community is sought on a wrong basis, the intensity of the search for it issues in conflict and disintegration. In such a world the church is called to be in its own life that fellowship which binds men together in their common dependence on God and overleaps all barriers of social status, race or nationality.

In consonance with its nature as true community, the church will call the nations to order their lives as members of the one family of God. The universal church, surveying the nations of the world, in every one of which it is now planted and rooted, must pronounce a condemnation of war unqualified and unrestricted. War can occur only as a fruit and manifestation of sin. This truth is unaffected by any question of what may be the duty of a nation which has to choose between entry upon war and a course which it believes to be a betrayal of right, or what may be the duty of a Christian citizen whose country is involved in war. The condemnation of war stands, and also the obligation to seek the way of freeing mankind from its physical, moral and spiritual ravages. If war breaks out, then preeminently the church must manifestly be the church, still united as the one body of Christ, though the nations wherein it is planted fight one another, consciously offering the same prayers that God's name may be hallowed, his kingdom come, and his will be done in both, or all, the warring nations. This fellowship of prayer must at all costs remain unbroken. The church must also hold together in one spiritual fellowship those of its members who take different views concerning their duty as Christian citizens in time of war.

To condemn war is not enough. Many situations conceal the fact of conflict under the guise of outward peace. Christians must do all in their power to promote among the nations justice and peaceful cooperation, and the means of peaceful adjustment to altering conditions. Especially should Christians in more fortunate countries press the demand for justice on behalf of the less fortunate. The insistence upon justice must express itself in a demand for such mitigation of the sovereignty of national states as is involved in the abandonment by each of the claim to be judge in its own cause.

We recognize the state as being in its own sphere the highest authority. It has the God-given aim in that sphere to uphold law and order and to minister to the life of its people. But as all authority is from God, the state stands under his judgment. God is himself the source of justice, of which the state is not lord but servant. The Christian can acknowledge no ultimate authority but God; his loyalty to the state is part of his loyalty to God and must never usurp the place of that primary and only absolute loyalty.

The church has duties laid upon it by God which at all cost it must perform, among which the chief is to proclaim the word of God and to make disciples, and to order its own life in the power of the Spirit dwelling in it. Because this is its duty it must do it, whether or not the state consents; and the state on its side should recognize the duty and assure full liberty for its performance. The church can claim such liberty for itself only as it is also concerned for the rights and liberties of others.

In the economic sphere the first duty of the church is to insist that economic activities, like every other department of human life, stand under the judgment of Christ. The existence of economic classes presents a barrier to human fellowship which cannot be tolerated by the Christian conscience. Indefensible inequalities of opportunity in regard to education, leisure and health continue to prevail. The ordering of economic life has tended to enhance acquisitiveness and to set up a false standard of economic and social success. The only forms of employment open to many men and women, or the fact that none is open, prevent them from finding a sense of Christian vocation in their daily life.

We are witnessing new movements which have arisen in reaction to these evils but which combine with their struggle for social justice the repudiation of all religious faith. Aware of the reality of sin, the church knows that no change in the outward ordering of life can of itself eradicate social evil. The church therefore cannot surrender to the utopian expectations of these movements, and their godlessness it must unequivocally reject; but in doing so it must recognize that Christians in their blindness to the challenging evils of the economic order have been partly responsible for the antireligious character of these movements.

Christians have a double duty—both to bear witness to their faith within the existing economic order and also to test all economic institutions in the light of their understanding of God's will. The forces of evil against which Christians have to contend are found not only in the hearts of men as individuals, but have entered into and infected the structure of society, and there also must be combated. The responsibility of the church is to insist on the true relationship of spiritual and economic goods. Man cannot live without bread, and man cannot live by bread alone. Our human wealth consists in fellowship with God and in him with our brethren. To this fellowship the whole economic order must be made subservient.

The questions which have mainly engaged the attention of the conference are questions that can be effectively dealt with, in practice, only by the laity. Those who are responsible for the daily conduct of industry, administration and public life must discover for themselves what is the right decision in an endless variety of concrete situations. If they are to receive the help they need in making responsible Christian decisions new types of ministry will have to be developed by the church.

The fulfillment of the tasks to which the church is called today lies largely in the hands of youth. Many loud voices are calling on young people to give themselves to political and social ideals, and it is often hard for them to hear the voice of Jesus Christ who calls them to be servants of the eternal kingdom. Yet many of the younger generation, often in spite of ridicule and sometimes of persecution, are turning to him, and individually as well as in Christian youth movements devote themselves to the renewal of the life of the churches and to making known the good news of Christ by word and action. We rejoice in their brave witness.

In the education of youth the church has a twofold task. First, it must be eager to secure for every citizen the fullest possible opportunity for the development of the gifts that God has bestowed on him. In particular, the church must condemn inequality of educational opportunity as a main obstacle to fullness of fellowship in the life of the community.

While the church is thus concerned with all education it has, also, a special responsibility to realize its own understanding of the meaning and end of education in the relation of life to God. In education, as elsewhere, if God is not recognized he is ignored. The church must claim the liberty to give a Christian education to its own children. It is in the field of education that the conflict between Christian faith and non-Christian conceptions of the ends of life, between the church and an all-embracing community life which claims to be the source and goal of every human activity, is in many parts of the world most acute. In this conflict all is at stake, and the church must gird itself for the struggle.

As we look to the future it is our hope and prayer that the Spirit of God may cause new life to break forth spontaneously in a multitude of different centers, and that there may come into being a large number of "cells" of Christian men and women associated in small groups for the discovery of fresh ways in which they may serve God and their fellow men.

We have deeply felt the absence from our fellowship of the churches that have not been represented at the conference. Our hearts are filled with anguish as we remember the suffering of the church in Russia. Our sympathy and gratitude go out to our Christian brethren in Germany; we are moved to a more living trust by their steadfast witness to Christ and we pray that we may be given grace to bear the same clear witness to the Lord.

We have much to encourage us since the conference at Stockholm twelve years ago. The sense of the unity of the church in all the world grows stronger every year. We trust that this cause will be yet more fully served by the world council of churches, proposals for which have been considered by the conference and commended to the churches.

We have tried during these days at Oxford to look without illusion at the chaos and disintegration of the world, the injustices of the social order and the menace and horror of war. The world is anxious and bewildered and full of pain and fear. We are troubled, yet we do not despair. Our hope is anchored in the living God. In Christ, and in the union of man with God and of man with man, which he creates, life even in face of all these evils has a meaning. In his name we set our hands as the servants of God, and in him of one another, to the task of proclaiming God's message of redemption, of living as his children and of combating injustice, cruelty and hate. The church can be of good cheer; it hears its Lord saying, "I have overcome the world."

*This "affirmation," while not yet naming the characteristics
of visible unity, served as an influential basis for subsequent
efforts.*[1]

Affirmation of Union in Allegiance to Our Lord Jesus Christ

Second World Conference on Faith and Order, Edinburgh, 1937

We are one in *faith* in our Lord Jesus Christ, the incarnate Word of God. We are one in allegiance to Him as Head of the Church, and as King of kings and Lord of lords. We are one in acknowledging that this allegiance takes precedence of any other allegiance that may make claims upon us.

This unity does not consist in the agreement of our minds or the consent of our wills. It is founded in Jesus Christ Himself, Who lived, died and rose again to bring us to the Father, and Who through the Holy Spirit dwells in His Church. We are one because we are all the objects of the love and grace of God, and called by Him to witness in all the world to His glorious gospel.

Our unity is of heart and spirit. We are divided in the outward forms of our life in Christ, because we understand differently His will for His Church. We believe, however, that a deeper understanding will lead us towards a united apprehension of the truth as it is in Jesus.

We humbly acknowledge that our divisions are contrary to the will of Christ, and we pray God in His mercy to shorten the days of our separation and to guide us by His Spirit into fullness of unity.

We are thankful that during recent years we have been drawn together; prejudices have been overcome, misunderstandings removed,

---

[1]Leonard Hodgson, ed., *The Second World Conference on Faith and Order, Edinburgh, 1937* (London: SCM Press, 1938), 275–76.

and real, if limited, progress has been made towards our goal of a common mind.

In this Conference we may gratefully claim that the Spirit of God has made us willing to learn from one another, and has given us a fuller vision of the truth and enriched our spiritual experience.

We have lifted up our hearts together in prayer; we have sung the same hymns; together we have read the same Holy Scriptures. We recognise in one another, across the barriers of our separation, a common Christian outlook and a common standard of values. We are therefore assured of a unity deeper than our divisions.

We are convinced that our unity of spirit and aim must be embodied in a way that will make it manifest to the world, though we do not yet clearly see what outward form it should take.

We believe that every sincere attempt to co-operate in the concerns of the kingdom of God thaws the severed communions together in increased mutual understanding and goodwill. We call upon our fellow-Christians of all communions to practise such co-operation; to consider patiently occasions of disunion that they may be overcome; to be ready to learn from those who differ from them; to seek to remove those obstacles to the furtherance of the gospel in the non-Christian world which arise from our divisions; and constantly to pray for that unity which we believe to be our Lord's will for His Church.

We desire also to declare to all men everywhere our assurance that Christ is the one hope of unity for the world in face of the distractions and dissensions of this present time. We know that our witness is weakened by our divisions. Yet we are one in Christ and in the fellowship of His Spirit. We pray that everywhere, in a world divided and perplexed, men may turn to Jesus Christ our Lord, Who makes us one in spite of our divisions; that He may bind in one those who by many *worldly* claims are set at variance; and that the world may at last find peace and unity in Him; to Whom be glory for ever.

Appendix 5

This message still stands, a half century after its formulation, as an eloquent statement of the vision behind the WCC. Its most famous phrase—"We intend to stay together"—was suggested by Kathleen Bliss, the only woman among the assembly's main speakers.[1]

Message

First Assembly of the WCC, Amsterdam, 1948

The World Council of Churches, meeting at Amsterdam, sends this message of greeting to all who are in Christ, and to all who are willing to hear.

We bless God our Father, and our Lord Jesus Christ Who gathers together in one the children of God that are scattered abroad. He has brought us here together at Amsterdam. We are one in acknowledging Him as our God and Saviour. We are divided from one another not only in matters of faith, order and tradition, but also by pride of nation, class and race. But Christ has made us His own, and He is not divided. In seeking Him we find one another. Here at Amsterdam we have committed ourselves afresh to Him, and have covenanted with one another in constituting this World Council of Churches. We intend to stay together. We call upon Christian congregations everywhere to endorse and fulfill this covenant in their relations one with another. In thankfulness to God we commit the future to Him.

When we look to Christ, we see the world as it is—His world, to which He came and for which He died. It is filled both with great hopes and also with disillusionment and despair. Some nations are rejoicing in new freedom and power, some are bitter because freedom is denied them, some are paralysed by division, and everywhere there is an undertone of fear. There are millions who are hungry, millions who have

---

[1] *Man's Disorder and God's Design,* The Amsterdam Assembly Series (New York: Harper, 1949), unnumbered pages at the end of the volume.

no home, no country and no hope. Over all mankind hangs the peril of total war. We have to accept God's judgment upon us for our share in the world's guilt. Often we have tried to serve God and mammon, put other loyalties before loyalty to Christ, confused the Gospel with our own economic or national or racial interests, and feared war more than we have hated it. As we have talked with one another here, we have begun to understand how our separation has prevented us from receiving correction from one another in Christ. And because we lacked this correction, the world has often heard from us not the Word of God but the words of men.

But there is a word of God for our world. It is that the world is in the hands of the living God, Whose will for it is wholly good; that in Christ Jesus, His incarnate Word, Who lived and died and rose from the dead, God has broken the power of evil once for all, and opened for everyone the gate into freedom and joy in the Holy Spirit; that the final judgment on all human history and on every human deed is the judgment of the merciful Christ; and that the end of history will be the triumph of His Kingdom, where alone we shall understand how much God has loved the world. This is God's unchanging Word to the world. Millions of our fellow men have never heard it. As we are met here from many lands, we pray God to stir up His whole Church to make this Gospel known to the whole world, and to call on all men to believe in Christ, to live in His love and to hope for His coming.

Our coming together to form a World Council will be vain unless Christians and Christian congregations everywhere commit themselves to the Lord of the Church in a new effort to seek together, where they live, to be His witnesses and servants among their neighbours. We have to remind ourselves and all men that God has put down the mighty from their seats and exalted the humble and meek. We have to learn afresh together to speak boldly in Christ's name both to those in power and to the people, to oppose terror, cruelty and race discrimination, to stand by the outcast, the prisoner and the refugee. We have to make of the Church in every place a voice for those who have no voice, and a home where every man will be at home. We have to learn afresh together what is the duty of the Christian man or woman in industry, in agriculture, in politics, in the professions and in the home. We have to ask God to teach us together to say No and to say Yes in truth. No to all that flouts the love of Christ, to every system, every programme and every person that treats any man as though he were an irresponsible thing or a means of profit, to the defenders of injustice in the name of order, to those who sow the seeds of war or urge war as inevitable; Yes, to all that conforms to the love of Christ, to all who seek for justice, to the peacemakers, to all who hope, fight and suffer for the cause of man, to all who—even without knowing it—look for new heavens and a new earth wherein dwelleth righteousness.

It is not in man's power to banish sin and death from the earth, to create the unity of the Holy Catholic Church, to conquer the hosts of Satan. But it is within the power of God. He has given us at Easter the certainty that His purpose will be accomplished. But, by our acts of obedience and faith, we can on earth set up signs which point to the coming victory. Till the day of that victory our lives are hid with Christ in God, and no earthly disillusion or distress or power of hell can separate us from Him. As those who wait in confidence and joy for their deliverance, let us give ourselves to those tasks which lie to our hands, and so set up signs that men may see.

Now unto Him that is able to do exceeding abundantly above all that we ask or think, according to the power that worketh in us, unto Him be glory in the Church by Christ Jesus, throughout all ages, world without end.

The formation of the WCC, and the holding of its first assembly did not answer a number of fundamental questions about the nature of the Council and its relationship to the member churches. That task was left to the WCC's central committee at its meeting in 1950, with the following result.[1]

The Church, the Churches, and the World Council of Churches

WCC Central Committee, Toronto, 1950

I. Introduction

The first Assembly at Amsterdam adopted a resolution on "the authority of the Council" which read:

The World Council of Churches is composed of churches which acknowledge Jesus Christ as God and Saviour. They find their unity in him. They do not have to create their unity; it is the gift of God. But they know that it is their duty to make common *cause* in the search for the expression of that unity in work and in life. The Council desires to serve the churches which are its constituent members as an instrument whereby they may bear witness together to their common allegiance to Jesus Christ, and cooperate in matters requiring united action. But the Council is far from desiring to usurp any of the functions which already belong to its constituent churches, or to control them, or to legislate for them, and indeed is prevented by its constitution from doing so. Moreover, while earnestly seeking fellowship in thought and action for all its members, the Council disavows

---

[1]W. A. Visser't Hooft, *The Genesis and Formation of the World Council of Churches* (Geneva: WCC, 1982), 112–20.

any thought of becoming a single unified church structure independent of the churches which have joined in constituting the Council, or a structure dominated by a centralized administrative authority.

The purpose of the Council is to express its unity in another way. Unity arises out of the love of God in Jesus Christ, which, binding the constituent churches to him, binds them to one another. It is the earnest desire of the Council that the churches may be bound closer to Christ and therefore closer to one another. In the bond of his love, they will desire continually to pray for one another and to strengthen one another, in worship and in witness, bearing one another's burdens and so fulfilling the law of Christ.

This statement authoritatively answered some of the questions which had arisen about the nature of the Council. But it is clear that other questions are now arising and some attempt to answer them must be made, especially in the face of a number of false or inadequate conceptions of the Council which are being presented.

II. The need for *further* statement

The World Council of Churches represents a new and unprecedented approach to the problem of interchurch relationships. Its purpose and nature can be easily misunderstood. So it is salutary that we should state more clearly and definitely what the World Council is and what it is not.

This more precise definition involves certain difficulties. It is not for nothing that the churches themselves have refrained from giving detailed and precise definitions of the nature of the Church. If this is true of them, it is not to be expected that the World Council can easily achieve a definition which has to take account of all the various ecclesiologies of its member churches. The World Council deals in a provisional way with divisions between existing churches, which ought not to be, because they contradict the very nature of the Church. A situation such as this cannot be met in terms of well-established precedents. The main problem is how one can formulate the ecclesiological implications of a body in which so many different conceptions of the Church are represented, without using the categories or language of one particular conception of the Church.

In order to clarify the notion of the World Council of Churches it will be best to begin by a series of negations so as to do away at the outset with certain misunderstandings which may easily arise or have already arisen, because of the newness and unprecedented character of the underlying conception.

III. What the World Council of Churches is not

1. **The World Council of Churches is not and must never become a superchurch.**

   It is not a superchurch. It is not the world church. It is not the Una Sancta of which the Creeds speak. This misunderstanding arises again and again although it has been denied as clearly as possible in official pronouncements of the Council. It is based on complete ignorance of the real situation within the Council. For if the Council should in any way violate its own constitutional principle, that it cannot legislate or act for its member churches, it would cease to maintain the support of its membership.

   In speaking of "member churches", we repeat a phrase from the Constitution of the World Council of Churches; but membership in the Council does not in any sense mean that the churches belong to a body which can make decisions for them. Each church retains the constitutional right to ratify or to reject utterances or actions of the Council. The "authority" of the Council consists only "in the weight which it carries with the churches by its own wisdom" (William Temple).

2. **The purpose of the World Council of Churches is not to negotiate unions between churches, which can only be done by the churches themselves acting on their own initiative, but to bring the churches into living contact with each other and to promote the study and discussion of the issues of Church unity.**

   By its very existence and its activities the Council bears witness to the necessity of a clear manifestation of the oneness of the Church of Christ. But it remains the right and duty of each church to draw from its ecumenical experience such consequences as it feels bound to do on the *basis* of its own convictions. No church, therefore, need fear that the Council will press it into decisions concerning union with other churches.

3. **The World Council cannot and should not be based on any one particular conception of the Church. It does not prejudge the ecclesiological problem.**

It is often suggested that the dominating or underlying conception of the Council is that of such a church or such and such a school of theology. It may well be that at a certain particular conference or in a particular utterance one can find traces of the strong influence of a certain tradition or theology.

The Council as such cannot possibly become the instrument of one confession or school without losing its very *raison d'être*. There is room and space in the World Council for the ecclesiology of every church which is ready to participate in the ecumenical conversation and which takes its stand on the Basis of the Council, which is "a fellowship of churches which accept our Lord Jesus Christ as God and Saviour".

4. Membership in the World Council of Churches does not imply that a church treats its own conception of the Church as merely relative.

There are critics, and not infrequently friends, of the ecumenical movement who criticize or praise it for its alleged inherent latitudinarianism. According to them the ecumenical movement stands for the fundamental equality of all Christian doctrines and conceptions of the Church and is, therefore, not concerned with the question of truth. This misunderstanding is due to the fact that ecumenism has in the minds of these persons become identified with certain particular theories about unity, which have indeed played a role in ecumenical history, but which do not represent the common view of the movement as a whole, and have never been officially endorsed by the World Council.

5. Membership in the World Council does not imply the acceptance of a specific doctrine concerning the nature of Church unity.

The Council stands for Church unity. But in its midst there are those who conceive unity wholly or largely as a full consensus in the realm of doctrine, others who conceive of it primarily as sacramental communion based on common church order, others who consider both indispensable, others who would only require unity in certain fundamentals of faith and order, again others who conceive the one Church exclusively as a universal spiritual fellowship, or hold that visible unity is inessential or even undesirable. But none of these conceptions can be called the ecumenical theory. The whole point of the ecumenical conversation is precisely that all these conceptions enter into dynamic relations with each other.

In particular, membership in the World Council does not imply acceptance or rejection of the doctrine that the unity of the Church consists in the unity of the invisible Church. Thus the statement in the Encyclical *Mystici Corporis* concerning what it considers the error of a spiritualized conception of unity does not apply to the World Council. The World Council does not "imagine a church which one cannot see or touch, which would be only spiritual, in which numerous Christian bodies, though divided in matters of faith, would nevertheless be united through an invisible link". It does, however, include churches which believe that the Church is essentially invisible as well as those which hold that visible unity is essential.

IV. The assumptions underlying the World Council of Churches

We must now try to define the positive assumptions which underlie the World Council of Churches and the ecclesiological implications of membership in it.

1. **The member churches of the Council believe that conversation, cooperation and common witness of the churches must be based on the common recognition that Christ is the Divine Head of the Body.**

The Basis of the World Council is the acknowledgment of the central fact that "other foundation can no man lay than that is laid even Jesus Christ". It is the expression of the conviction that the Lord of the Church is God-among-us who continues to gather his children and to build his Church himself.

Therefore, no relationship between the churches can have any substance or promise unless it starts with the common submission of the churches to the headship of Jesus Christ in his Church. From different points of view churches ask: "How can men with opposite convictions belong to one and the same federation of the faithful?" A clear answer to that question was given by the Orthodox delegates in Edinburgh 1937 when they said: "in spite of all our differences, our common Master and Lord is *one*—Jesus Christ who will lead us to a more and more close collaboration for the edifying of the Body of Christ." The fact of Christ's headship over his people compels all those who acknowledge him to enter into real and close relationships with each other—even though they differ in many important points.

2. The member churches of the World Council believe on the basis of the New Testament that the Church of Christ is one.

The ecumenical movement owes its existence to the fact that this article of the faith has again come home to men and women in many churches with an inescapable force. As they face the discrepancy between the truth that there is and can only be one Church of Christ, and the fact that there exist so many churches which claim to be churches of Christ but are not in living unity with each other, they feel a holy dissatisfaction with the present situation. The churches realize that it is a matter of simple Christian duty for each church to do its utmost for the manifestation of the Church in its oneness, and to work and pray that Christ's purpose for his Church should be fulfilled.

3. The member churches recognize that the membership of the Church of Christ is more inclusive than the membership of their own church body. They seek, therefore, to enter into living contact with those outside their own ranks who confess the Lordship of Christ.

All the Christian churches, including the Church of Rome, hold that there is no complete identity between the membership of the Church Universal and the membership of their own church. They recognize that there are church members "extra muros", that these belong "aliquo modo" to the Church, or even that there is an "ecclesia extra ecclesiam". This recognition finds expression in the fact that with very few exceptions the Christian churches accept the baptism administered by other churches as valid.

But the question arises what consequences are to be drawn from this teaching. Most often in church history the churches have only drawn the negative consequence that they should have no dealings with those outside their membership. The underlying assumption of the ecumenical movement is that each church has a positive task to fulfill in this realm. That task is to seek fellowship with all those who, while not members of the same visible body, belong together as members of the mystical body. And the ecumenical movement is the place where this search and discovery take place.

4. The member churches of the World Council consider the relationship, of other churches to the Holy Catholic Church which the Creeds profess as a subject for mutual

consideration. Nevertheless, membership does not imply that each church must regard the other member churches as churches in the true and full sense of the word.

There is a place in the World Council both for those churches which recognize other churches as churches in the full and true sense, and for those which do not. But these divided churches, even if they cannot yet accept each other as true and pure churches, believe that they should not remain in isolation from each other, and consequently they have associated themselves in the World Council of Churches.

They know that differences of faith and order exist, but they recognize one another as serving the one Lord, and they wish to explore their differences in mutual respect, trusting that they may thus be led by the Holy Spirit to manifest their unity in Christ.

5. **The member churches of the World Council recognize in other churches elements of the true Church. They consider that this mutual recognition obliges them to enter into a serious conversation with each other in the hope that these elements of truth will lead to the recognition of the full truth and to unity based on the full truth.**

It is generally taught in the different churches that other churches have certain elements of the true Church, in some traditions called "vestigia ecclesiae". Such elements are the preaching of the Word, the teaching of the Holy Scriptures and the administration of the sacraments. These elements are more than pale shadows of the life of the true Church. They are a fact of real promise and provide an opportunity to strive by frank and brotherly intercourse for the realization of a fuller unity. Moreover, Christians of all ecclesiological views throughout the world, by the preaching of the Gospel, brought men and women to salvation by Christ, to newness of life in him, and into Christian fellowship with one another.

The ecumenical movement is based upon the conviction that these "traces" are to be followed. The churches should not despise them as mere elements of truth but rejoice in them as hopeful signs pointing towards real unity. For what are these elements? Not dead remnants of the past but powerful means by which God works. Questions may and must be raised about the validity and purity of teaching and sacramental life, but there can be no question that such dynamic elements of church life justify the hope that the churches which maintain them will be led into full truth. It is through the ecumenical conversation that this recognition of truth is facilitated.

6. **The member churches of the Council are willing to consult together in seeking to learn of the Lord Jesus Christ what witness he would have them to bear to the world in his name.**

Since the very *raison d'être* of the Church is to witness to Christ, churches cannot meet together without seeking from their common Lord a common witness before the world. This will not always be possible. But when it proves possible thus to speak or act together, the churches can gratefully accept it as God's gracious gift that in spite of their disunity he has enabled them to render one and the same witness and that they may thus manifest something of the unity, the purpose of which is precisely "that the world may believe", and that they may "testify that the Father has sent the Son to be the Saviour of the world".

7. **A further practical implication of common membership in the World Council is that the member churches should recognize their solidarity with each other, render assistance to each other in case of need, and refrain from such actions as are incompatible with brotherly relationship.**

Within the Council the churches seek to deal with each other with a brotherly concern. This does not exclude extremely frank speaking to each other, in which within the Council the churches ask each other searching questions and face their differences. But this is to be done for the building up of the Body of Christ. This excludes a purely negative attitude of one church to another. The positive affirmation of each church's faith is to be welcomed, but actions incompatible with brotherly relationship towards other member churches defeat the very purpose for which the Council has been created. On the contrary, these churches should help each other in removing all obstacles to the free exercise of the Church's normal functions. And whenever a church is in need or under persecution, it should be able to count on the help of the other churches through the Council.

8. **The member churches enter into spiritual relationships through which they seek to learn from each other and to give help to each other in order that the Body of Christ may be built up and that the life of the churches may be renewed.**

It is the common teaching of the churches that the Church as the temple of God is at the same time a building which has been built and a building which is being built. The Church has, therefore, aspects which belong to its very structure and essence and cannot be changed. But it has other aspects which are subject to change. Thus the life of the Church, as it expresses itself in its witness to its own members *and* to the world, needs constant renewal. The churches can and should help each other in this realm by a mutual exchange of thought and of experience. This is the significance of the study work of the World Council and of many other of its activities. There is no intention to impose any particular pattern of thought or life upon the churches. But whatever insight has been received by one or more churches is to be made available to all the churches for the sake of the "building up of the Body of Christ".

None of these positive assumptions, implied in the existence of the World Council, is in conflict with the teachings of the member churches. We believe therefore that no church need fear that by entering into the World Council it is in danger of denying its heritage.

As the conversation between the churches develops and as the churches enter into closer contact with each other, they will no doubt have to face new decisions and problems. For the Council exists to break the deadlock between the churches. But in no case can or will any church be pressed to take a decision against its own conviction or desire. The churches remain wholly free in the action which, on the basis of their convictions and in the light of their ecumenical contacts, they will or will not take.

A very real unity has been discovered in ecumenical meetings which is, to all who collaborate in the World Council, the most precious element of its life. It exists and we receive it again and again as an unmerited gift from the Lord. We praise God for this foretaste of the unity of his people and continue hopefully with the work to which he has called us together. For the Council exists to serve the churches as they prepare to meet their Lord who knows only one flock.

The New Delhi statement is one of the most famous—and longest!—sentences in ecumenical history. It remains the definitive expression of "organic unity."[1]

Report of the Section on Unity
Third Assembly of the WCC, New Delhi, 1961

I. The Church's unity

1. The love of the Father and the Son in the unity of the Holy Spirit is the source and goal of the unity which the Triune God wills for all men and creation. We believe that we share in this unity in the Church of Jesus Christ, who is before all things and in whom all things hold together. In him alone, given by the Father to be Head of the Body, the Church has its true unity. The reality of this unity was manifest at Pentecost in the gift of the Holy Spirit, through whom we know in this present age the first fruits of that perfect union of the Son with his Father, which will be known in its fullness only when all things are consummated by Christ in his glory. The Lord who is bringing all things into full unity at the last is he who constrains us to seek the unity which he wills for his Church on earth here and now.

2. We believe that the unity which is both God's will and his gift to his Church is being made visible as all in each place who are baptized into Jesus Christ and confess him as Lord and Saviour are brought by the Holy Spirit into one fully committed fellowship, holding the one apostolic faith, preaching the one Gospel, breaking the one bread, joining in common prayer and having a corporate life reaching out in witness and service to all and who at the same time are united with the whole Christian fellowship in all places and all ages in such wise that ministry and members are accepted by all, and that all can act and speak together as occasion requires for the tasks to which God calls his people.

---

[1] W. A. Visser't Hooft, ed., *The New Delhi Report: The Third Assembly of the World Council of Churches* (London: SCM Press, 1962), 116–25.

It is for such unity that we believe we must pray and work.

3. This brief description of our objective leaves many questions unanswered. We are not yet of a common mind on the interpretation and the means of achieving the goal we have described. We are clear that unity does not imply simple uniformity of organization, rite or expression. We all confess that sinful self-will operates to keep us separated and that in our human ignorance we cannot discern clearly the lines of God's design for the future. But it is our firm hope that through the Holy Spirit God's will as it is witnessed to in Holy Scripture will be more and more disclosed to us and in us. The achievement of unity will involve nothing less than a death and rebirth of many forms of church life as we have known them. We believe that nothing less costly can finally suffice...

All in each place

7. This statement uses the word 'place' both in its primary sense of local neighbourhood and also, under modern conditions, of other areas in which Christians need to express unity in Christ. Thus being one in Christ means that unity among Christians must be found in each school where they study, in each factory or office where they work and in each congregation where they worship, as well as between congregations. 'Place' may further imply not only local communities but also wider geographical areas such as states, provinces or nations, and certainly refers to all Christian people in each place regardless of race and class...

Fully committed fellowship

10. The word 'fellowship' *(koinonia)* has been chosen because it describes what the Church truly is. 'Fellowship' clearly implies that the Church is not merely an institution or organization. It is a fellowship of those who are called together by the Holy Spirit and in baptism confess Christ as Lord and Saviour. They are thus 'fully committed' to him and to one another. Such a fellowship means for those who participate in it nothing less than a renewed mind and spirit, a full participation in common praise and prayer, the shared realities of penitence and forgiveness, mutuality in suffering and joy, listening together to the same Gospel, responding in faith, obedience and service, joining in the one mission of Christ in the world, a self-forgetting love for all for whom Christ died, and the reconciling grace which breaks down every wall of race, colour, caste, tribe, sex, class and nation. Neither does this 'fellowship' imply a rigid uniformity of structure, organization or

government. A lively variety marks corporate life in the one Body of one Son...

A corporate life reaching out

15. Mission and service belong to the whole Church. God calls the Church to go out into the world to witness and serve in word and deed to the one Lord Jesus Christ, who loved the world and gave himself for the world. In the fulfilment of our missionary obedience the call to unity is seen to be imperative, the vision of one Church proclaiming one Gospel to the whole world becomes more vivid and the experience and expression of our given unity more real. There is an inescapable relation between the fulfilment of the Church's missionary obligation and the recovery of her visible unity...

In all places and all ages

17. Every church and every Christian belongs to Christ. Because we belong to him we are bound through him to the Church and the Christians in all places and all ages. Those who are united in each place are at the same time one with believers in all places. As members of the one Body they share both in each other's joys and sufferings. The Church as a universal fellowship means also that we are part of the People of God of all ages, and as such are one with Abraham, Isaac and Jacob, and all their descendants in the faith until the end of the age. Work for unity in Christ is continually attacked by all the evil forces which fear the light of truth and holiness and obscure our own vision also. We now see our unity only darkly, but we know that then we shall see it clearly when we see him face to face. But it is also our hope which gives us courage to expose our differences and our divisions and call upon God to reveal to us even now that which has hitherto been hidden from our eyes. We pray, with the praying Christ, that *all* may be one. To this end we must work while it is day...

Implications for local church life

19. The place where the development of the common life in Christ is most clearly tested is in the local situation, where believers live and work. There the achievements and the frustrations are most deeply felt; but there too the challenge is most often avoided. It is where we live and work together daily that our Lord's own test is most clearly imposed, 'by this shall all men know that ye are my disciples, if ye have love one to another'. Before and beneath all outward expression is the

commandment to love one another as he has loved us. As soon as we begin to obey this command, we can ignore each other no longer and we shall actively seek the means of giving expression to that love. The Lund Conference on Faith and Order in 1952 put out this challenge in the form of suggesting that Christians ought always to seek to do together everything which conscience did not compel them to do separately. Loyalty to conscience takes different forms in different traditions. In some churches, the rules of corporate discipline make very clear the limits of corporate action; in others there is a far greater area of free manoeuvre. But all of us must confess that, in the life of our churches at the local level, we are still far from being together in all those ways in which, with a good conscience, we might be. It will be through daily obedience in the paths that are already open to us that our eyes will be enlightened to the fuller vision of our life together. The disclosure of the goal is inseparable from the faithful walking in the way in which he leads us.

20. (a) There is need for an increase in opportunities of growing together as local churches: through common worship, Bible study groups, prayer cells, joint visitation, common witness in our communities. Locally as in the whole ecumenical movement we should be especially ready in Christian love to seek out and to establish fellowship with those traditions and minorities to which we are not now related. Even where we are compelled to remain separate at present in central aspects of the life of our congregations there is considerable freedom for developing areas of common worship, witness and service in homes and communities.

21. (b) Ordinary social life already brings men together into various associations—academic, professional, industrial, political, etc. Within these forms of unity there is need for a Christian unity of those who may learn from each other how to bear their witness in those settings. Ecumenical thought in the calling of the laity needs to be shared in groups of this kind and it has its own bearing on church unity, for denominational divisions are often found to be quite irrelevant on this frontier. What is the bearing of that discovery upon our inherited divisions?

22. (c) Sometimes Christians will find themselves in associations of this kind in situations where their witness will involve sharp conflict, and they may reach a point where they have to break with the association. Wherever such Conflicts arise, Christians are called to give their witness to a true expression of unity.

23. (d) Since much of this lay witness cuts across denominational lines, it clearly calls for united planning and execution as men and women

seek in a common discipline under Christ to express his Lordship over all life, drawing their local churches together in the process.

24. Our division at the Lord's Table may be most acutely felt at the local level, especially if Christians of separated church traditions are truly meeting each other in common obedience to Christ. Where they are content virtually to ignore each other as Christians, or where the ecclesiastical traditions raise no difficulty, the problem may not be felt. But this 'scandal' of eucharistic division appears at every one of the three levels we are considering. Since it is at the local level that it comes home most persistently, if it is seen at all, this is the point at which briefly to consider what the problem is, for there is no point at which we more completely fail to understand each other.

25. For some Christians, the Lord's own command 'Do this' is an imperative which over-rides all our divisions. If Holy Communion is the sovereign means of grace for the forgiveness and conquest of sin, then that is true of the sin of division as well. Thus it is intolerable and incomprehensible that a common love of God should not be expressed and deepened by common participation in the Holy Communion which he offers.

26. For some Christians, the essence of the Christian life is incorporation into the Body of Christ realized as fellowship in an organic and transcendent unity of faith, life and love made visible in a pattern of ministry and sacraments which is indivisible. Then it is intolerable and incomprehensible that those who do not share the organic life should expect to share in its eucharistic expression.

27. For neither view can there be any final peace so long as others who are known to be in Christ are not with us at the Holy Communion. But there are serious and deeply felt differences about how we should behave in our present recognition that God wills a unity which we do not manifest.

28. Although the problem may be most acutely felt at the local level, it is not at this level that it can find any general solution. Local churches may rightly ask, however, that confessional convictions be made clear amongst them if they are to be saved from uncomprehending suffering. In certain places groups of Christians have entered into intercommunion with full knowledge of the gravity of the issues involved. In these instances there has been, if not ecclesiastical approval, at least the withholding of disapproval. None of us can ignore the issues which such action raises. The Table is the Lord's gift before it is our blessing. We must therefore ask whether there are situations, e.g. during unity

negotiations, when intercommunion is possible even before full union is achieved, and all must feel with renewed intensity the agony of broken communion at the one Table of the Lord.

29. In the WCC we commit ourselves, in our local churches also, to an abiding concern for each other. In staying together we have discovered more and more that Christ is present among those to whom we cannot, on the grounds of our differing convictions, grant the full meaning of the word 'church'. If Christ is present with them, is he not calling us in ways we cannot yet clearly discern, to move out towards him in order that we may receive our full unity with him and with his people? When the real Christian encounter takes place locally we are forced to face these vital questions. This self-examination is always difficult; for we cannot and must not surrender those truths and ways of church life which we believe are God's will for his Church, and which the others do not yet accept. At the same time, we cannot and should not refuse to move out to Christ whose presence we recognize in the life of the others.

30. In this situation are we not constrained by the love of God to exert pressure on the limits of our own inherited traditions, recognizing the theological necessity of what we may call 'responsible risk'? We emphasize the word *responsible;* for such actions must be taken with sincere respect for our confessional position and with the full attempt to explore with the Christian communion to which we belong the meaning of what we are doing. Clearly also, the responsible risk will be different according to our different convictions. Nevertheless, unless there is this preparedness to seek for responsible ways of breaking through to fresh understandings, we cannot hope to be shown the way to that growing unity which we know to be God's will for us. Responsible use of local situations to explore such possibilities is a challenge in every place.

Appendix 8

This decree is "the official charter of the Roman Catholic Church's active participation in the one ecumenical movement."[1] The text was overwhelmingly approved by the church's bishops (2,137 to 11) during the third session of Vatican II.

Decree on Ecumenism of the Second Vatican Council, 1964

Introduction

1. The restoration of unity among all Christians is one of the principal concerns of the Second Vatican Council. Christ the Lord founded one Church and one Church only. However, many Christian Communions present themselves to men as the true inheritors of Jesus Christ; all indeed profess to be followers of the Lord but they *differ* in mind and go different ways, as if Christ Himself were divided (Cf. 1 Cor. 1,13). Certainly, such division openly contradicts the will of Christ, scandalizes the world, and damages that most holy cause, the preaching of the Gospel to every creature.

The Lord of Ages nevertheless wisely and patiently follows out the plan of His grace on our behalf, sinners that we are. In recent times He has begun to bestow more generously upon divided Christians remorse over their divisions and longing for unity.

Everywhere large numbers have felt the impulse of this grace, and among our separated brethren also there increases from day to day a movement, fostered by the grace of the Holy Spirit, for the restoration of unity among all Christians. Taking part in this movement, which is called ecumenical, are those who invoke the Triune God and confess Jesus as Lord and Savior. They do this not merely as individuals but

---

[1]Thomas F. Stransky, in *Doing the Truth in Charity,* ed. Thomas F. Stransky and John B. Sheerin (New York: Paulist Press, 1982), 18–26.

also as members of the corporate groups in which they have heard the Gospel, and which each *regards* as his Church and indeed, God's. And yet, almost everyone, though in different ways, longs for the one visible Church of God, a Church truly universal and sent forth to the whole world that the world may be converted to the Gospel and so be saved, to the glory of God.

The sacred Council gladly notes all this. It has already declared its teaching on the Church, and now, moved by a desire for the restoration of unity among all the followers of Christ, it wishes to set before all Catholics guidelines, helps and methods, by which they too can respond to the grace of this divine call.

1. Catholic Principles on Ecumenism

2. What has revealed the love of God among us is that the only-begotten Son of God has been sent by the Father into the world, so that, being made man, He might by His redemption of the entire human race give new life to it and unify it (Cf. 1 Jn. 4,9; Col. 1,18–20; Jn. 11,52). Before offering Himself up as a spotless victim upon the altar of the cross, He prayed to His Father for those who believe: "that they all may be one: even as thou, Father, art in me, and I in thee, that they also may be one in us, so that the world may believe that thou hast sent me" (Jn. 17,21). In His Church He instituted the wonderful sacrament of the Eucharist by which the unity of the Church is both signified and brought about. He gave His followers a new commandment to love one another (Cf. Jn. 13,34), and promised the Spirit, their Advocate (Cf. Jn. 16,7), who, as Lord and life-giver, should remain with them forever.

After being lifted up on the cross and glorified, the Lord Jesus poured forth the Spirit whom He had promised, and through whom He has called and gathered together the people of the New Covenant, which is the Church, into a unity of faith, hope and charity, as the Apostle teaches us: "There is one body and one Spirit, just as you were called to the one hope of your calling; one Lord, one faith, one baptism" (Eph. 4,4–5). For "all you who have been baptized into Christ have put on Christ...for you are all one in Christ Jesus" (Gal. 3,27–28). It is the Holy Spirit, dwelling in those who believe and pervading and ruling over the entire Church, who brings about that wonderful communion of the faithful and joins them together so intimately in Christ that He is the principle of the Church's unity. By distributing various kinds of spiritual gifts and ministries (Cf. 1 Cor. 12,4–11), He enriches the Church of Jesus

Christ with different functions "in order to equip the saints for the work of service, so as to build up the body of Christ" (Eph. 4,12).

In order to establish this His holy Church everywhere in the world till the end of time, Christ entrusted to the College of the Twelve the task of teaching, ruling and sanctifying (Cf. Mt. 28,18–20, in conjunction with Jn. 20,21–23). Among their number He chose Peter. And after his confession of faith, He determined that on him He would build His Church; to him He promised the keys of the kingdom of heaven (Cf. Mt. 16,19, in conjunction with Mt. 18,18), and after his profession of love, entrusted all His sheep to him to be confirmed in faith (Cf. Lk. 22,32) and shepherded in perfect unity (Cf. Jn. 21,15–18), with Himself, Christ Jesus, forever remaining the chief cornerstone (Cf. Eph. 2,20) and shepherd of our souls (Cf. 1 Pet. 2,25; 1 Vatican Council, Sess. IV [1870], The Constitution *Pastor Aeternus:* Coil. Lac. 7,482a).

It is through the faithful preaching of the Gospel by the Apostles and their successors—the bishops with Peter's successor at their head— through their administering the sacraments, and through their governing in love, that Jesus Christ wishes His people to increase, under the action of the Holy Spirit; and He perfects its fellowship in unity: in the confession of one faith, in the common celebration of divine worship, and in the fraternal harmony of the family of God.

The Church, then, God's only flock, like a standard high lifted for the nations to see it (Cf. Is. 11,10–12), ministers the Gospel of peace to all mankind (Cf. Eph. 2,17–18, in conjunction with Mk. 16,15), as it makes its pilgrim way in hope toward *its* goal: the fatherland above (Cf. 1 Pet. 1,3–9).

This is the sacred mystery of the unity of the Church, in Christ and through Christ, with the Holy Spirit energizing its various functions. The highest exemplar and source of this mystery is the unity, in the Trinity of Persons, of one God, the Father and the Son in the Holy Spirit.

3. In this one and only Church of God from its very beginnings there arose certain rifts (Cf. 1 Cor. 11,18–19; Gal. 1,6–9; 1 Jn. 2,18–19), which the Apostle strongly censures as damnable (Cf. 1 Cor. 1,11ff.; 11,22). But in subsequent centuries much more serious dissensions appeared and quite large Communities became separated from full communion with the Catholic Church for which, often enough, men of both sides were to blame. However, one cannot charge with the sin of the separation those who at present are born into these Communities and in them are brought up in the faith of Christ, and the Catholic Church accepts them

with respect and affection as brothers. For men who believe in Christ and have been properly baptized are brought into certain, though imperfect, communion with the Catholic Church. Without doubt, the differences that exist in varying degrees between them and the Catholic Church—whether in doctrine and sometimes in discipline, or concerning the structure of the Church—do indeed create many obstacles, sometimes serious ones, to full ecclesiastical communion. The ecumenical movement is striving to overcome these obstacles. But even in spite of them it remains true that all who have been justified by faith in baptism are incorporated into Christ (Cf. Council of Florence, Sess. VIII [1439], The Decree *Exultate Dec:* Mansi 31,1055A); they therefore have a right to be called Christians, and with good reason are accepted as brothers by the children of the Catholic Church (Cf. St. Augustine, *In Ps. 32, Enar. II, 29: PL* 36,299).

Moreover, some, even very many of the most significant elements and endowments, which together go to build up and give life to the Church itself, can exist outside the visible boundaries of the Catholic Church: the written Word of God; the life of grace; faith, hope and charity, with the other interior gifts of the Holy Spirit, as well as visible elements. All of these, which come from Christ and lead back to Him, belong by right to the one Church of Christ.

The brethren divided from us also carry out many liturgical actions of the Christian religion. In ways that vary according to the condition of each Church or Community, these most certainly can truly engender a life of grace, and, one must say, can aptly give access to the communion of salvation.

It follows that the separated Churches (Cf. IV Lateran Council [1215], Constitution IV: Mansi 22,990; II Council of Lyons [1274], Profession of faith of Michael Palaeologos: Mansi 24,71E; Council of Florence, Sess. VI [1439], Definition *Laetenur caeli:* Mansi 31,1026E) and Communities as such, though we believe they suffer from defects already mentioned, have been by no means deprived of significance and importance in the mystery of salvation. For the Spirit of Christ has not refrained from using them as means of salvation which derive their efficacy from the very fullness of grace and truth entrusted to the Catholic Church.

Nevertheless, our separated brethren, whether considered as individuals or as Communities and Churches, are not blessed with that unity which Jesus Christ wished to bestow on all those to whom He has given new birth into one body, and whom He has quickened to newness of life—that unity which the Holy Scriptures and the ancient Tradition of the Church proclaim. For it is through Christ's Catholic Church alone, which is the all-embracing means of salvation, that the fullness of the means of salvation can be obtained. It was to the apostolic college alone, of which Peter is the head, that we believe that our Lord entrusted all the blessings of the New Covenant, in order to establish on earth the one Body of Christ into which all those should be fully incorporated who belong in any way to the people of God. During its pilgrimage on earth, this people, though still in its members liable to sin, is growing in Christ and is guided by God's gentle wisdom, according to His hidden designs, until it shall happily arrive at the fullness of eternal glory, in the heavenly Jerusalem.

4. Today, in many parts of the world, under the inspiring grace of the Holy Spirit, many efforts are being made in prayer, word and action to attain that fullness of unity which Jesus Christ desires. The sacred Council exhorts, therefore, all the Catholic faithful to recognize the signs of the times and to take an active and intelligent part in the work of ecumenism.

The term "ecumenical movement" indicates the initiatives and activities encouraged and organized, according to the various needs of the Church and as opportunities offer, to promote Christian unity. These are: first, every effort to avoid expressions, judgments and actions which do not represent the condition of our separated brethren with truth and fairness and so make mutual relations with them more difficult. Then, "dialogue" between competent experts from different Churches and Communities; in their meetings, which are organized in a religious spirit, each explains the teaching of his Communion in greater depth and brings out clearly its distinctive features. Through such dialogue everyone gains a truer knowledge and more just appreciation of the teaching and religious life of both Communions. In addition, these Communions engage in that more intensive cooperation in carrying out any duties for the common good of humanity which are demanded by every Christian conscience. They also come together for common prayer, where this is permitted. Finally, all are led to examine their own faithfulness to Christ's will for the Church and, wherever necessary, undertake with vigor the task of renewal and reform.

Such actions, when they are carried out by the Catholic faithful with prudent patience and under the attentive guidance of their bishops, promote justice and truth, concord and collaboration, as well as the spirit of brotherly love and unity. The result will be that, little by little, as the obstacles to perfect ecclesiastical communion are overcome, all Christians will be gathered, in a common celebration of the Eucharist, into the unity of the one and only Church, which Christ bestowed on His Church from the beginning. This unity, we believe, subsists in the Catholic Church as something she can never lose, and we hope that it will continue to increase until the end of time.

However, it is evident that the work of preparing and reconciling those individuals who wish for full Catholic communion is of its nature distinct from ecumenical action. But there is no opposition between the two, since both proceed from the marvelous ways of God.

In ecumenical work, Catholics must assuredly be concerned for their separated brethren, praying for them, keeping them informed about the Church, making the first approaches toward them. But their primary duty is to make a careful and honest appraisal of whatever needs to be renewed and done in the Catholic household itself, in order that its life may bear witness more clearly and faithfully to the teachings and institutions which have been handed down from Christ through the Apostles.

For although the Catholic Church has been endowed with all divinely revealed truth and with all means of grace, yet its members fail to live by them with all the fervor that they should. As a result the radiance of the face shines less brightly in the eyes of our separated brethren and of the world at large, and the growth of God's kingdom is retarded. Every Catholic must therefore aim at Christian perfection (Cf. James 1,4; Rom. 12,1–2) and, each according to his station, play his part that the Church, which bears in her own body the humility and dying of Jesus (Cf. 2 Cor. 4,10; Phil. 2,5–8), may daily be more purified and renewed, against the day when Christ will present her to Himself in all her glory without spot or wrinkle (Cf. Eph. 5,27).

While preserving unity in essentials, let everyone in the Church, according to the office entrusted to him, preserve a proper freedom in the various forms of spiritual life and discipline, in the variety of liturgical rites, and even in the theological elaborations of revealed truth. In all things let charity prevail. If they are true to this course of action, they will be giving ever richer expression to the authentic catholicity of the Church.

On the other hand, Catholics must gladly acknowledge and esteem the truly Christian endowments from our common heritage which are to be found among our separated brethren. It is right and salutary to recognize the riches of Christ and virtuous works in the lives of others who are bearing witness to Christ, sometimes even to the shedding of their blood. For God is always wonderful in His works and worthy of all praise.

Nor should we forget that anything wrought by the grace of the Holy Spirit in the hearts of our separated brethren can contribute to our own edification. Whatever is truly Christian is never contrary to what genuinely belongs to the faith; indeed, it can always bring a more perfect realization of the very mystery of Christ and the Church.

Nevertheless, the divisions among Christians prevent the Church from realizing the fullness of catholicity proper to her in those of her Sons who, though joined to her by baptism, are yet separated from full communion with her. Furthermore, the Church herself finds it more difficult to express in actual life her full catholicity in all its aspects.

This sacred Council is gratified to note that the participation by the Catholic faithful in ecumenical work is growing daily. It commends this work to the bishops everywhere in the world for their diligent promotion and prudent guidance.

2. The Practice of Ecumenism

5. The concern for restoring unity involves the whole Church, faithful and clergy alike. It extends to everyone, according to the talent of each, whether it be exercised in daily Christian living or in theological and historical studies. This concern itself already reveals to some extent the bond of brotherhood existing among all Christians and it leads toward full and perfect unity, in accordance with what God in His kindness wills.

6. Every renewal of the Church (Cf. V Lateran Council, Sess. XII [1517], Constitution *Constitzaj:* Mansi 32,98 SB-C) essentially consists in an increase of fidelity to her own calling. Undoubtedly this explains the dynamism of the movement toward unity.

Christ summons the Church, as she goes her pilgrim way, to that continual reformation of which she always has need, insofar as she is an institution of men here on earth. Consequently, if, in various times and circumstances, there have been deficiencies in moral conduct or in church discipline, or even in the way that church teaching has been formulated—to be carefully distinguished from the deposit of faith itself—these should be set right at the opportune moment and in the proper way.

Church renewal therefore has notable ecumenical importance. Already this renewal is taking place in various spheres of the Church's life: the biblical and liturgical movements, the preaching of the Word of God and catechetics, the apostolate of the laity, new forms of religious life and the spirituality of married life, and the Church's social teaching and activity. All these should be considered as promises and guarantees for the future progress of ecumenism.

7. There can be no ecumenism worthy of the name without interior conversion. For it is from newness of attitudes of mind (Cf. Eph. 4,23), from self-denial and unstinted love, that desires of unity take their rise and develop in a mature way. We should therefore pray to the Holy Spirit for the grace to be genuinely self-denying, humble, gentle in the service of others and to have an attitude of brotherly [and sisterly] generosity toward them. The Apostle of the Gentiles says: "I, therefore, a prisoner for the Lord, beg you to lead a life worthy of the calling to which you have been called, with all humility and meekness, with patience, forbearing one another in love, eager to maintain the unity of the spirit in the bond of peace" (Eph. 4,1–3). This exhortation is directed especially to those raised to sacred orders in order that the mission of Christ may be continued. He came among us—"not to be served but to serve" (Mt. 20,28).

St. John has testified: "if we say we have not sinned, we make Him a liar, and His word is not in us" (1 Jn. 1,10). This holds good for sins against unity. Thus, in humble prayer we beg pardon of God and of our separated brethren, just as we forgive them that trespass against us.

The faithful should remember that they are better promoting union among Christians, indeed living it better, the more they strive to live holier according to the Gospel.

For the closer their union with the Father, the Word, and the Spirit, the more deeply and easily will they be able to grow in mutual brotherly love.

8. This change of heart and holiness of life, along with public and private prayer for the unity of Christians, should be regarded as the soul of the whole ecumenical movement, and merits the name, "spiritual ecumenism."

It is a recognized custom for Catholics to meet for frequent recourse to that prayer for the unity of the Church with which the Savior Himself on the eve of His death so fervently appealed to His Father: "That they may all be one" (Jn. 17,21).

In certain special circumstances, such as in prayer services "for unity" and during ecumenical gatherings, it is allowable, indeed desirable that Catholics should join in prayer with their separated brethren. Such prayers in common are certainly a very effective means of petitioning for the grace of unity, and they are a genuine expression of the ties which still bind Catholics to their separated brethren. "For where two or three are gathered together in my name, there am I in the midst of them" (Mt. 18,20).

Yet worship in common *(communicatio in sacris)* is not to be considered as a means to be used indiscriminately for the restoration of unity among Christians. There are two main principles upon which the practice of such common worship depends: first, that of the unity of the Church which ought to be expressed; and second, that of the sharing in means of grace. The expression of unity very generally forbids common worship. Grace to be obtained sometimes commends it. The concrete course to be adopted, when due regard has been given to all the circumstances of time, place and persons, is left to the prudent decision of the local episcopal authority, unless the Bishops' Conference according to its own statutes, or the Holy See, has determined otherwise.

9. We must get to know the outlook of our separated brethren. Study is absolutely required for this, and it should be pursued in fidelity to truth and with a spirit of good will. Catholics, who already have a proper grounding, need to acquire a more adequate understanding of the respective doctrines of our separated brethren, their history, their spiritual and liturgical life, their religious psychology and cultural background. Most valuable for this purpose are meetings of the two sides—especially for discussion of theological problems—where each can treat with the other on an equal footing, provided that those who take part in them under the guidance of the authorities are truly competent. From such dialogue will emerge still more clearly what the situation of the Catholic Church really is. In this way, too, we will better understand the outlook of our separated brethren and more aptly present our own belief.

10. Sacred theology and other branches of knowledge, especially those of an historical nature, must be taught with due regard also for the ecumenical point of view, so that they may correspond as exactly as possible with the facts.

It is important that future pastors and priests should have mastered a theology that has been carefully worked out in this way and not polemically, especially with regard to those aspects which concern the relations of separated brethren with the Catholic Church. For it is the formation which priests receive upon which so largely depends the necessary instruction and spiritual formation of the faithful and of religious.

Moreover, Catholics engaged in missionary work in the same territories as other Christians ought to know, particularly in these times, the problems and the benefits which affect their apostolate because of the ecumenical movement.

11. The manner and order in which Catholic belief is expressed should in no way become an obstacle to dialogue with our brethren. It is, of course, essential that the doctrine be clearly presented in its entirety. Nothing is so foreign to the spirit of ecumenism as a false irenicism which harms the purity of Catholic doctrine and obscures its assured genuine meaning.

At the same time, Catholic belief must be explained more profoundly and precisely, in such a way and in such terms as our separated brethren can also really understand it.

Furthermore, in ecumenical dialogue, Catholic theologians, standing fast by the teaching of the Church yet searching together with separated brethren into the divine mysteries, should do so with love for the truth, with charity, and with humility. When comparing doctrines with one another, they should remember that in Catholic doctrine there exists an order or "hierarchy" of truths, since they vary in their relation to the foundation of the Christian faith. Thus the way will be opened whereby this kind of "fraternal rivalry" will incite all to a deeper realization and a clearer expression of the unfathomable riches of Christ (Cf. Eph. 3,8).

12. Before the whole world let all Christians confess their faith in God, one and three, in the incarnate Son of God, our Redeemer and Lord. United in their efforts, and with mutual respect, let them bear witness to our common hope which does not play us false. Since cooperation in social matters is so widespread today, all men without exception are called to work together; with much greater reason are all those who believe in God, but most of all, all Christians in that they bear the seal of Christ's name. Cooperation among Christians vividly expresses that bond which already unites them, and it sets in clearer relief the features of Christ the Servant. Such cooperation, which has already begun in many countries, should be developed more and more, particularly in regions where a social and technical evolution is taking place. It should contribute to a just appreciation of the dignity of the human person, to the promotion of the blessings of peace, the application of Gospel principles to social life, and the advancement of the arts and sciences in a truly Christian spirit. It should also be intensified in the use of every possible means to relieve the afflictions of our times, such

as famine and natural disasters, illiteracy and poverty, lack of housing, and the unequal distribution of wealth. Through such cooperation, all believers in Christ are able to learn easily how they can understand each other better and esteem each other more, and how the road to the unity of Christians may be made smooth.

This statement marks the conclusion of a Faith and Order study project on "The Unity of the Church and the Unity of Mankind," the WCC's first systematic attempt to relate these themes. Numerous subsequent studies have drawn inspiration from this brief report.[1]

Towards Unity in Tension
WCC Commission on Faith and Order, 1974

1. In pursuing our quest for the visible unity of the Church, we are seeking the fulfilment of God's purpose as it is declared to us in Jesus Christ. This purpose concerns the world, the whole of mankind, and the whole created order. Christ has been lifted up to draw all men to himself, and as all things have been created through him and all men are made in his image, so it is his will that all should be reconciled in him through the "blood of the Cross" (Col. 1:20).

Our concern for the unity of the Church is, therefore, held within a concern for that wider and fuller unity whereof we believe the Church is called to be a sign, first-fruit, and instrument.

Thus it is as part of our faith that we say: "The Church is bold in speaking of itself as the sign of the coming unity of mankind" [the Uppsala assembly, 1968].

2. But in a time when human inter-relatedness has become oppressive for so many, can we speak of "the unity of mankind"? When liberation and struggle have become a vocation for the oppressed, is it enough to speak of "signs" and "church unity"? What does "unity" require of Christians in situations of human conflict?

3. When we speak of the unity of mankind, we intend to refer to more than the unity of the Church. We speak in the light of the new

---

[1]Günther Gassmann, ed., *Documentary History of Faith and Order 1968–1993,* Faith and Order paper no. 1S9 (Geneva: WCC, 1993), 144–47.

creation of the human unity in and for which God created mankind, and which he has promised to his children in his Kingdom. It will come in God's own time and power, in judgment and fulfilment, and will be the final definition and realization of mankind's hope for unity.

4. This unity, whose foretaste we know in the Spirit, demands and enables in history the just interdependence of free people, societies, and nations. It is this just interdependence of which mankind has dreamed, of which its laws and ideologies attempt to speak, and which it continually struggles to attain and protect. Movements of liberation, for instance, derive a large part of their motivation from the sense of solidarity of man with man in the fight for justice and equality. Although this just interdependence is not identical with "the *unity* of mankind", it is also not separable from it. In this light, humanity's search for a just interdependence is in reality a hunger, implanted by the Creator, a hunger for which Christians share a mutual responsibility with all human beings.

It is part of that travail in which the whole creation groans, longing for liberation (Rom. 8:19–22). It is that longing which Christians share, sustained in it by the work of the Spirit. Therefore, Christians have a mandate for critical, loyal participation in humanity's strivings for a more adequate human community. They are also called to recognize, proclaim, and expect God's judgment upon all forms of that community which are unjust and oppressive.

5. Mankind's yearning for a just interdependence is magnified today by certain historical factors and forces which are producing an inevitable, fast-developing human inter-relatedness and organization. In speaking of this developing "human inter-relatedness", we intend to refer to a fact of modern life which has both positive and negative aspects.

6. On the positive side, a providential increase in the human ability for just interdependence is taking place. World-wide economic structures, mass communication, the development of science and technology, international travel–to name only a few factors–increasingly inter-relate us in one another's economics, societies, politics, cultures, aspirations. They provide a basis for vastly strengthening the just interdependence of free people. We understand this inter-relatedness as extending not only in space but in time. We are increasingly linked with the heritage of past generations and projected into new responsibilities for generations unborn. This makes it all the more urgent and possible to act now to reverse the crisis of our environment and stem the reckless exploitation of this earth's resources.

7. But the unity of mankind—as the Bible teaches us—bears the mark of Cain. From the beginning, human wickedness has made human history a scene of hostility and alienation. The human quest for a just interdependence is vitiated by sinful self-assertion. In the name of unity and interdependence false structures are created, marked by false dependence and oppression. The powerful exploit the weak in the name of unity. The commercial and financial structures which bind the world together also oppress and enslave. Race oppresses race, and even the Church itself uses its power to subject others to a false unity. Hence it may be more accurate to speak of human brokenness than of mankind's unity.

This universal hostility and alienation has been exposed and condemned in the Cross of Jesus Christ. It is that Cross—the Cross of the one who is risen and who reigns—which marks the birth of a new humanity recreated in him. It gives us our belief in and our hope for the unity of mankind.

8. We believe that the unity of mankind for which we pray and hope, and the just interdependence of free people inseparable from it, cannot be thought of apart from God's liberating activity and an active human response and participation. Moreover, this liberation is indivisible: it concerns the human soul, mind, and body, and no less mankind in its cultures, societies, and politics. It must confront, struggle against, and overcome whatever alienates human beings from themselves, from each other, and from God. We are aware of limits to liberation which will never be overcome as long as history lasts. The powers of sickness and death will always be present and there will always be suffering people calling for solidarity and love. In recognizing it, our hope in the liberating power of God's Kingdom is reinforced. We are called to that unity where "there shall be an end to death, and to mourning and crying and pain" (Rev. 21:4). And, therefore, we are called to face the problems of suffering and conflict not simply as an unpleasantness to be avoided, or as a disorder to be suppressed, but also as a necessary implication of liberation.

9. We recognize that once men become involved in the struggles for liberation, two factors emerge. A sense of solidarity springs up among those involved together in a common task. But other relationships are strained, even broken, by such engagement. But there is no other way of achieving a just interdependence than by facing the issues, engaging in encounter, and even conflict.

10. How does such conflict affect the unity of the Church? What does it mean for the goal of the visible unity of the Church? Christians have a vocation to be the fellowship of reconciliation. But Christians involved in the struggle for liberation in fact often find themselves closer to others who share the struggle with them, Christian or not, than to other Christians who are not committed to it. This problem cannot be avoided. An ecclesiastical unity which would stand in the way of struggles for liberation would be a repressive unity, hindering the just interdependence which Christians are called to serve. We are learning that Church unity can be a "unity in tension".

11. Christian faith trusts the reality of grace in which it is empowered to bear the tensions of conflicts. Jesus Christ accepted the necessity of conflict, yet transcended it in his death on the Cross. He took upon himself the cost of conflict; forces of divisions are finally overcome in the unity which Christ creates and gives, as he leads all things to unity in himself. The Church has also been given remarkable anticipations of this unity, even in the midst of severe conflict. The Church must, therefore, bear the tension of conflicts within itself, and so fulfil its ministry of reconciliation, in obedience to the Lord who chooses to sacrifice himself rather than to confer on the forces of division any ultimate authority. The Church accordingly is called to work for unity, through suffering, under the sign of the Cross.

12. The Church is called to be a visible sign of the presence of Christ, who is both hidden and revealed to faith, reconciling and healing human alienation in the worshipping community. The Church's calling to be such a sign includes struggle and conflict for the sake of the just interdependence of mankind.

There is here an enduring tension which will not be resolved until the promise is fulfilled of a new heaven and a new earth. Until that day we have to accept the fact that we do not fully know how to embody in the life of the nations and communities of our time the unity which God wills. There is only one foundation for human unity—the new Man, Jesus Christ. But what we build on that foundation will be tested by fire, and may not pass the test.

We must resolutely refuse any too easy forms of unity, or any misuse of the "sign", that conceal a deeper disunity. At the same time, we may believe in and give witness to our unity in Christ, even with those from whom we may, for his sake, have to part. This means to be prepared to be a "fellowship in darkness"—dependent on the guidance of the Holy Spirit for the form which our fellowship should seek and take; and a "unity in tension"–dependent on the Spirit for the strength to reconcile within the one body of the Church all whom the forces of disunity would otherwise continue to drive apart. For there is no "fellowship in darkness" without some sign of the reconciling judgment and love of Christ.

This is the latest in a series of important statements on the meaning of unity produced by WCC assemblies since 1961. It was first written by the Faith and Order commission at the request of the WCC's central committee.[1]

The Unity of the Church as Koinonia: Gift and Calling

Seventh Assembly of the WCC, Canberra, 1991

1.1. The purpose of God according to holy scripture is to gather the whole of creation under the Lordship of Christ Jesus in whom, by the power of the Holy Spirit, all are brought into communion with God (Eph. 1). The church is the foretaste of this communion with God and with one another. The grace of our Lord Jesus Christ, the love of God, and the communion of the Holy Spirit enable the one church to live as sign of the reign of God and servant of the reconciliation with God, promised and provided for the whole creation. The purpose of the church is to unite people with Christ in the power of the Spirit, to manifest communion in prayer and action and thus to point to the fullness of communion with God, humanity and the whole creation in the glory of the kingdom.

1.2. The calling of the church is to proclaim reconciliation and provide healing, to overcome divisions based on race, gender, age, culture, colour, and to bring all people into communion with God. Because of sin and the misunderstanding of the diverse gifts of the Spirit, the churches are painfully divided within themselves and among each other. The scandalous divisions damage the credibility of their witness to the world in worship and service. Moreover they contradict not only the church's witness but also its very nature.

---

[1] *Documentary History of Faith and Order 1963–1993, 3–5.*

1.3. We acknowledge with gratitude to God that in the ecumenical movement the churches walk together in mutual understanding, theological convergence, common suffering and common prayer, shared witness and service as they draw close to one another. This has allowed them to recognize a certain degree of communion already existing between them. This is indeed the fruit of the active presence of the Holy Spirit in the midst of all who believe in Christ Jesus and who struggle for visible unity now. Nevertheless churches have failed to draw the consequences for their life from the degree of communion they have already experienced and the agreements already achieved. They have remained satisfied to co-exist in division.

2.1. The unity of the church to which we are called is a koinonia given and expressed in the common confession of the apostolic faith; a common sacramental life entered by the one baptism and celebrated together in one eucharistic fellowship; a common life in which members and ministries are mutually recognized and reconciled; and a common mission witnessing to the gospel of God's grace to all people and serving the whole of creation. The goal of the search for full communion is realized when all the churches are able to recognize in one another the one, holy, catholic and apostolic church in its fullness. This full communion will be expressed on the local and the universal levels through conciliar forms of life and action. In such communion churches are bound in all aspects of their life together at all levels in confessing the one faith and engaging in worship and witness, deliberation and action.

2.2. Diversities which are rooted in theological traditions, various cultural, ethic or historical contacts are integral to the nature of communion; yet there are limits to diversity. Diversity is illegitimate when, for instance, it makes impossible the common confession of Jesus Christ as God and Saviour the same yesterday, today and forever (Heb. 13:8); and salvation and the final destiny of humanity as proclaimed in holy scripture and preached by the apostolic community. In communion diversities are brought together in harmony as gifts of the Holy Spirit, contributing to the richness and fullness of the church of God.

3.1. Many things have been done and many remain to be done on the way towards the realization of full communion. Churches have reached agreements in bilateral and multilateral dialogues which are already bearing fruit, renewing their liturgical and spiritual life and their theology. In taking specific steps together the churches express and encourage the enrichment and renewal of Christian life, as they learn from one another, work together for justice and peace, and care together for God's creation.

3.2. The challenge at this moment in the ecumenical movement as a reconciling and renewing movement towards full visible unity is for the seventh assembly of the WCC to call all churches:

- to recognize each other's baptism on the basis of the BEM document;

- to move towards the recognition of the apostolic faith as expressed through the Nicene-Constantinopolitan Creed in the life and witness of one another;

- on the basis of convergence in faith in baptism, eucharist and ministry to consider, wherever appropriate, forms of eucharistic hospitality; we gladly acknowledge that some who do not observe these rites share in the spiritual experience of life in Christ;

- to move towards a mutual recognition of ministries;

- to endeavour in word and deed to give common witness to the gospel as a whole;

- to recommit themselves to work for justice, peace and the integrity of creation, linking more closely the search for the sacramental communion of the church with the struggles for justice and peace;

- to help parishes and communities express in appropriate ways locally the degree of communion that already exists.

4.1. The Holy Spirit as promoter of koinonia (2 Cor. 13:13) gives to those who are still divided the thirst and hunger for full communion. We remain restless until we grow together according to the wish and prayer of Christ that those who believe in him may be one (John 17:21). In the process of praying, working and struggling for unity, the Holy Spirit comforts us in pain, disturbs us when we are satisfied to remain in our division, leads us to repentance, and grants us joy when our communion flourishes.

Appendix 11

Our Ecumenical Vision
Eighth Assembly of the WCC, Harare, 1998

At the [World Council of Churches'] recommitment service on 13 December 1998, delegates reaffirmed their ecumenical vision using the following text:

Jesus Christ, who has called us to be one, is in our midst! As Christians from every part of the world, we give thanks that the triune God has drawn our churches closer together in faith and life, witness and service.

We celebrate the 50th anniversary of the World Council of Churches–"a fellowship of churches which confess the Lord Jesus Christ as God and Saviour according to the scriptures and therefore seek to fulfil together their common calling to the glory of the one God, Father, Son and Holy Spirit".

Receiving the legacy of those who have gone before us:

We are drawn by the vision of a church
that will bring all people into communion with God and with
    one another,
professing one baptism, celebrating one holy communion, and
    acknowledging a common ministry.
We are drawn by the vision of a church
which will express its unity by confessing the apostolic faith,
living in conciliar fellowship, acting together in mutual
    accountability.
We are challenged by the vision of a church
That will reach out to everyone, sharing, caring, proclaiming the
    good news of God's redemption,
a sign of the kingdom and a servant of the world.

We are challenged by the vision of a church,
The people of God on the way together, confronting all
    divisions of race, gender, age or culture, striving to realize
    justice and peace, upholding the integrity of creation.

Affirming anew that our task is to embody, here and now, the vision of what God's people are called to be:

We journey together as a people freed by God's forgiveness. In
    the midst of the brokenness of the world,
We proclaim the good news of reconciliation, healing and justice
    in Christ.
We journey together as a people with resurrection faith. In the
    midst of exclusion and despair,
We embrace, in joy and hope, the promise of life in all its
    fullness.
We journey together as a people of prayer. In the midst of
    confusion and loss of identity,
We discern signs of God's purpose being fulfilled and expect the
    coming of God's reign.

Therefore, this is our vision for the ecumenical movement:

We long for the visible oneness of the body of Christ,
affirming the gifts of all,
young and old, women and men, lay and ordained.

We expect the healing of human community,
the wholeness of God's entire creation.

We trust in the liberating power of forgiveness,
transforming enmity into friendship
and breaking the spiral of violence.

We open ourselves for a culture of dialogue and solidarity,
sharing life with strangers
and seeking encounter with those of other faiths.

This is our commitment:

*We intend to stay together and are restless to grow together in unity. We
respond to the prayer of Jesus Christ*

that all may be one in order that the world may believe
   (John 17:21).
We are sustained by the assurance
that in God's purpose all things shall be united in Christ–things
   in heaven and things on earth (Ephesians 1:10).
We affirm that what unites us is stronger than what separates us.
Neither failures nor uncertainties, neither fears nor threats
will weaken our intention to continue to walk together on the
   way to unity,
welcoming those who would join us on this journey,
widening our common vision discovering new ways of
   witnessing.
and acting together in faith.
We recommit ourselves in this 50th anniversary year to strengthen the
   World Council of Churches
as a truly ecumenical fellowship, fulfilling the purposes for
   which it was founded–to the glory of the triune God.

Prayer

God of unity, God of love, what we say with our lips, make
   strong in our hearts, what we affirm with our minds, make
   vivid in our lives. Send us your Spirit
to pray in us what we dare not pray,
to claim us beyond our own claims,
to bind us when we are tempted to go our own ways. Lead us
   forward.
Lead us together. Lead us to do your will, the will of Jesus
   Christ, our Lord. Amen.

Printed in the United States
200119BV00010B/412-477/A